Against All Odds

Against All Odds

Walter Tull – The Black Lieutenant

by
Stephen Wynn

Pen & Sword
MILITARY

First published in Great Britain in 2018 by
Pen & Sword Military
an imprint of
Pen & Sword Books Ltd
47 Church Street
Barnsley
South Yorkshire
S70 2AS

ISBN 978 1 52670 404 7

Printed and bound in England
by TJ International Ltd, Padstow, Cornwall

Pen & Sword Books Ltd incorporates the Imprints of Pen & Sword Archaeology,
Atlas, Aviation, Battleground, Discovery, Family History, History, Maritime,
Military, Naval, Politics, Railways, Select, Transport, True Crime, Fiction,
Frontline Books, Leo Cooper, Praetorian Press, Seaforth Publishing, Wharncliffe
and White Owl.

For a complete list of Pen & Sword titles please contact
PEN & SWORD BOOKS LIMITED
47 Church Street, Barnsley, South Yorkshire, S70 2AS, England
E-mail: enquiries@pen-and-sword.co.uk
Website: www.pen-and-sword.co.uk

Dedication

Whilst writing this book a friend's wife sadly passed away after losing her battle with cancer. I would like to dedicate this book in her memory:

Julie Hopton 25 October 1958 – 24 October 2016
Gone from this world, but remembered for ever more.

Contents

About the Author

Stephen is a retired police officer having served with Essex Police as a constable for thirty years between 1983 and 2013. He is married to Tanya and has two sons, Luke and Ross, and a daughter, Aimee. His sons served five tours of Afghanistan between 2008 and 2013 and both were injured. This led to the publication of his first book, *Two Sons in a Warzone – Afghanistan: The True Story of a Father's Conflict*, published in October 2010.

Both Stephen's grandfathers served in and survived the First World War, one with the Royal Irish Rifles, the other in the Mercantile Marine, whilst his father was a member of the Royal Army Ordnance Corps during the Second World War.

Stephen collaborated with Ken Porter on a book published in August 2012, *German PoW Camp 266 – Langdon Hills*. It spent six weeks as the number one best-selling book in Waterstones, Basildon between March and April 2013. They have also collaborated on other books in this local history series.

Stephen has also co-written three crime thrillers, published between 2010 and 2012, which centre round a fictional detective named Terry Danvers.

Against All Odds: Walter Tull the Black Lieutenant is one of numerous books which Stephen has written for Pen and Sword on aspects of the Great War, including several in the Towns and Cities of The Great War series which commemorate the sacrifices made by young men up and down the country.

Introduction

Walter Daniel John Tull was many things to many people, but above all else he was a determined individual who, in his comparatively short life, fought against adversity, inequality and racism.

He was a passionate man who gave one hundred per cent to everything that he did. In some aspects black people faced very difficult times throughout the United Kingdom at the end of the nineteenth and at the beginning of the twentieth centuries. For a black person to get on in life was not easy; Walter Tull was one of those who managed to do so. His sporting prowess opened many doors for him, but that did not mean that he had it easy, far from it. During his footballing career, not only did he have to deal with the sometimes vitriolic crowd abuse from away fans, but opposing players spent most of the game trying to kick lumps out of him, in a day and age when football boots were more akin to a pair of heavy Dr Martens 'bovver boots', than the ultra light, multi-coloured footwear of today's footballers.

The 2001 Census records that there were more than one million black people living in the United Kingdom, with just one per cent of the entire population describing themselves as being 'Black Caribbean'. This was broken down further to 0.8 per cent classing themselves as 'Black African', and 0.2 per cent being 'Black other'. It would be fair to say that the 1901 version of the United Kingdom which Walter Tull found himself growing up in, consisted of very few black people, in fact the colour of a person's skin or their ethnicity, wasn't even one of the ten categories included in the 1901 Census, more than likely because it was either assumed that nearly everybody living in the United Kingdom at that time was either white, or those who were not, accounted for such a small percentage, it was deemed not worth recording.

Walter proved, by way of example, that a man, no matter what the colour of his skin, or his social standing in society, could achieve most things in life if he wanted it badly enough and if he applied himself in the right way. Despite coming from a poor, immigrant family and losing both parents at a relatively young age, he went on to become a professional footballer, representing both Tottenham Hotspur and Northampton Town football clubs, as well as becoming a professional soldier in the British Army.

He was only the third black man to play professional football in the top flight of the English Football league, in what is now the Premiership, and he became the first black officer to lead white troops into battle, during the Great War of 1914 – 1919.

Soon after the outbreak of the war, and despite being a regular in Northampton Town's football team at the time, he was one of the first footballers to enlist and go off and fight. For him, it was never going to be a case of waiting around to be called up. He enlisted initially in the Army as a private soldier in the 17th (1st Football) Battalion, Middlesex Regiment. He quickly worked his way through the ranks, and in May 1917 he was commissioned as a second lieutenant in the same regiment.

He was a principled man who knew what he had to do, and he died doing what he believed in. A truly remarkable individual who was admired and respected by nearly everybody who got to know him as a person, and who could see past the colour of his skin.

Chapter 1

Daniel Tull's story and Walter's early life

The story begins in Barbados with the birth of Walter's father Daniel Tull. Barbados, a sovereign country situated in the Lesser Antilles, in the Americas, is a small island, only 21 miles in length and 14 miles across. Its size helped foster a tight-knit community amongst those who lived there.

The island was first settled by the English in 1627, later becoming first an English and then subsequently a British colony. The *Olive Blossom*, a trading ship owned by English merchant William Courteen and commanded by Captain John Powell, had first landed at the island's St James Town in 1625, claiming it in the name of King James 1.

The main crops grown on the island had originally been ginger, indigo, cotton and tobacco, these items were added to in 1640 with the beginning of the sugar cane industry, and with it came an increased use of slave labour, but not just from the African continent. Initially much of the labour force was European, coming in from all over Britain, and over the course of time this also included prisoners of war, vagrants picked up off of the streets of the United Kingdom, forcibly transported to Barbados, and then sold as servants to the rich land owners.

The island's population in 1644 was estimated to be in the region of some 30,000 people, more than 29,000 of whom were of some kind of British descent, with those of African descent being measured in the hundreds. At the time of emancipation in Barbados in 1833, the slave population alone was estimated to have been in the region of 83,000. In 1854, two years before the birth of Walter's father, Daniel, there was an outbreak of cholera, which claimed the lives of more than 20,000 of the island's inhabitants.

Daniel was born in Barbados in 1856, twenty-three years after the abolition of slavery in the Caribbean, but his father had been a slave before he became a free man at the time of the emancipation. On leaving school, Daniel chose carpentry as his way of earning a living, initially becoming an apprentice carpenter, for which the wages were modest. He struggled to make ends meet, but was determined to make a better life for himself, so it was with this in mind that at the age of 20, he found passage on a ship that was sailing to England. After a six-week journey across the Atlantic Ocean, in what would have been a cramped sailing ship, the vessel docked at Folkestone, Kent, in the late summer of 1876.

Rather than remaining on the ship as its carpenter, Daniel decided to try his luck in Folkestone and went looking for work. Although a popular harbour town from which many big ships regularly arrived and departed, having a black man living in their midst wasn't a common event for the local population. But with his carpentry skills in demand and the ability to both read and write an additional bonus, Daniel found more than enough work to provide him with sufficient money to rent a room, buy clothes and feed himself.

He was a regular churchgoer, attending each Sunday at the town's Grace Hill Wesleyan Chapel, and it was where he met and fell in love with a local girl, Alice Elizabeth Palmer, who lived at 86 Street End Farm, Hougham, Kent, with her parents, Stephen and Sarah Palmer, and her two brothers, Richard and John Palmer, who like their father, were both farm labourers.

Four years after his arrival in England, Daniel and Alice were married in February 1880 at Folkestone. The first census in which they appear together is in 1881, and shows the newly weds living at 8 Garden Street, Folkestone, as yet without children, although six would follow – William, born in 1882, Cecilia, born in 1884, Edward born in 1887, Walter born in 1888, and finally, Elsie, who was born in 1891.

What the census did not record was that Daniel and Alice's first child, a daughter Bertha, who was born on 9 February 1881, died when she was only five weeks old, in March 1881, never having appeared on the census. Infant deaths were common at the time.

Walter Daniel John Tull, was born in Folkestone, Kent, on 28 April 1888, to parents Daniel and Alice Tull. Daniel was black and Alice was white, and even though such mixed marriages were rare at the time, Alice's parents warmly welcomed Daniel in to their family.

The 1891 Census shows Daniel, Alice, and four of their children, William (9), Cecilia, (7), Edward (4), and Walter (2), all living at number 51 Walton Road, Folkestone, which was a pleasant working class, family area where nearly all of the men had physically demanding jobs, such as labourers, gardeners, carpenters, plumbers, glaziers or stone masons.

It would be fair to say, taking into account the social expectations of the time, that Daniel, Alice and their family, had a reasonably good life. The three Tull brothers all attended the nearby North Board Elementary School, which today is the Mundella Primary School, at a time when the Education Act 1880 meant compulsory school attendance for all children up to and including the age of ten. This was raised to the age of eleven in 1893, with truancy still being a real issue, as many parents needed their children to be out at work earning a much-needed income for the family.

Daniel found more than enough work to provide a roof over their heads and for sufficient food and clothes for the entire family, whilst Alice was the wife, mother and home maker. She gave birth to another daughter, Elsie, born in 1891, but Alice sadly died in May 1895 after a long battle with cancer. She was just 42 years of age. This left the newly widowed Daniel having to juggle his work commitments with the responsibilities of having to look after five young children all under the age of 14. Thankfully for Daniel he was able to rely on Alice's family for help with his children, and Alice's niece, Clara Alice Susanna Palmer, came to stay and help care for them so that Daniel could carry on working and keep his family together.

On 17 October 1896, Daniel married Clara. Their daughter, Miriam, was born in November 1897, but the following month, on 10 December

1897, Daniel died of heart disease. With Miriam only a month old, Clara suddenly found herself with six children to care for, without the money or the accommodation to be able to do so. The Tull children had, in a very short time, gone from being part of a loving tight-knit family unit, to having lost both of their parents in quick succession. Despite having a caring stepmother in Clara, they would very soon be split up as she simply was not able to keep them together. So it was that on 24 February 1898 Walter and Edward, who were 8 and 10 years of age respectively, found themselves in a children's home in the East End of London. It must have been a massive shock for the two boys, moving from the fresh air and seaside community of Folkestone to the poverty and degradation of the East End of London, with its smog, overcrowding and almost constant hustle and bustle of one of the world's major capital cities.

Walter's family were Methodists, and it was through friends at her local Methodist church in Folkestone that Clara managed to make arrangements to have Walter and his younger brother, Edward, accepted in to the Methodist-run Bonner Road Children's Home, in Bethnal Green. A letter was sent to the Reverend Stephenson, the man who ran the orphanage. The following is taken from an entry on spartacus-educational.com: '*The father of these children was a negro and they are consequently coloured children. I do not know if you are aware of this or whether it will in any way affect the application.*'

The Reverend Stephenson replied to the letter which had been sent to him by the Eltham Union, explaining that the colour of the boy's skin made absolutely no difference, but that the orphanage would only be willing and able to accept the boys if the Eltham Union would contribute towards the boys' upkeep. This was agreed, the required financing was found and Walter and Edward were accepted by the orphanage. It would have been an extremely tough decision for Clara to make, as she would have known full well that once the boys left her care and were accepted into the home, it was highly unlikely she would ever be able to claim them back again, because of the financial penalty that she would have to pay to reimburse the orphanage.

The wording of the agreement between the orphanage and the parents or the next of kin of the child entering the home was as follows:

'It should be distinctly understood by the persons signing this Form of Agreement that they thereby give the Committee the power to send the child to any situation in this country or abroad. This does not imply that the child will actually be sent out of the country, but the Committee claim the right to exercise their power if, when the time comes for the child to leave the Home, they consider its future welfare will be better secured by emigration.'

The Form of Agreement then had the parent's or next of kin's name entered followed by the name of the child entering the home.

'I hereby declare that my child enters The Children's Home with my full approval and consent, and I hereby commit him to the care of the Principal of the Home, and I pledge myself not to interfere with him in any way so long as he remains therein; and I hereby further agree to the Child being sent to any situation in this country or ABROAD, chosen by the said Principal. Also I promise to give every assistance in my power to the Principal and Officers in their efforts on the Child's behalf.

Further, I hereby agree not to remove the Child without the consent of the Committee, but should I do so I hereby agree to make payment to the Treasurer for the time being of the said Children's Home, of the outlay which shall have been expended by the Institution on the Child's behalf, at the rate of Eight Shillings per week from the time of admission.'

Clara would have had to sign two such forms when Walter and Edward were admitted to the Bonner Road Children's Home. It is clear to see that the longer a child remained in the home, the more difficult it would have been for a parent to reclaim them. With two boys in the Home, Clara was looking at a charge of sixteen shillings a week. These were simply not the sums of money that ordinary people could afford; in a time when people lived from one week's pay to the next, very few people had the ability to save.

Children's homes of the day could be strict, disciplined and regimented in their expectations, but such establishments had the physical, emotional, and educational wellbeing of the children under their care, at heart. They were clean and welcoming places, where the children were clothed, fed and generally well looked after. The other option didn't really bear thinking about. Many children who had either been orphaned or simply abandoned by their parents, had no option but to live, sleep and survive the best they could, on the streets. There was little or no protection from the elements, the only food they could get they either had to beg for or steal. The consequences of the latter choice could have fatal repercussions if they were caught. By being in such a home the children at least had some chance of making it through to adulthood, and have the skills and abilities to be able to provide for themselves, by acquiring a reasonably well paid job.

Although widely referred to as the Bonner Road Children's Home, a reference to the name of the road where it was located, the 1901 Census of England and Wales, records it as the Children's Home, Wesleyan Orphanage, near Victoria Park, Bethnal Green. The home had officially opened on 4 October 1871, and its secretary was Mr John Pendlebury. He was a kind and understanding man, even allowing his own daughter Sarah to marry one of the boys who had lived at the home as an 'inmate'. It was a well-run establishment which provided the children with both an education and, when they were deemed old enough, training in a trade which was provided on site, with the aim of furnishing them with the ability to find worthwhile work when they left.

The children were woken up at six o'clock each morning, followed by a roll call at six-thirty. Those who were training in a trade were sent to their workshops, whilst the younger ones carried out housework. Breakfast was at eight o'clock, followed by a service in the home's chapel at eight-thirty. The day then began by nine o'clock with lessons or work until five o'clock in the afternoon, with time for lunch and play. After dinner activities included swimming – the home had the luxury of its own pool – other sports, singing, lectures and other activities which were deemed to be of an 'instructive' nature. Lights out most evenings was at eight o'clock.

As neither of the brothers had ever travelled outside Folkestone before, they might have just as well been on the other side of the world as in Bethnal Green. One can only imagine how daunting and traumatic the whole experience must have been for them, losing both of their parents in the space of just two years, being forced to leave the only town they had ever known, and to then end up in a children's home miles away from where they lived. But at least they had the comfort of being with each other, well, at least until 14 November 1900 that was. Inexplicably the brothers were then split up when Edward was adopted by the Warnock family from Scotland and he went to live in Glasgow, but they kept in touch with each other despite their separation.

In August 1899, the boys' stepmother Clara married farm labourer William Charles Beer and the 1901 Census showed them living at 158 Little Singledge, Coldred, Dover, with her daughter Miriam and stepdaughter Elsie. By the time of the 1911 Census, William and Clara, along with Miriam, had moved to West View Valley Road, River near Dover. Clara's widowed father, William Palmer, was also living with them. Elsie, who by then was 19 years of age, had left home and was working as a live-in domestic servant for Mr and Mrs Samuel and Maria Buttler, also of West View Valley Road. Mr Buttler was 71 years of age and a retired marine engineer.

Edward's adoptive parents, James and Helen Warnock, were as loving and caring to him as if he were their own flesh and blood. James Warnock was a dentist by profession and when Edward was old enough, he was sent to the prestigious Royal College of Physicians and Surgeons in Glasgow, to study dentistry. The faculty had first been established in 1599. Edward qualified as a dentist in 1910 and although he applied for numerous positions, he quickly found that the colour of his skin could just as easily determine whether or not he acquired a position in a dental practice, rather than his qualifications and ability. Because of the prejudices which he faced he began working for his father.

On the day war broke out, 4 August 1914, James Warnock died of chronic nephritis, a kidney disease. He was 59 years of age. Edward took over his father's dental practice at 419 St Vincent Street, Glasgow, which was also the family home. It is quite possible that Edward inadvertently became the first black dentist in Britain.

On 28 September 1918, Edward married Elizabeth Hutchinson, it was a happy union which was blessed with a daughter, Jean who was born in 1929.

It was clear sporting prowess was not confined to Walter, as Edward had become quite an accomplished golfer, winning numerous amateur tournaments, including the Glasgow Dental Cup. He was also a notable singer with a particularly fine baritone voice.

An article on the website Spartacus-education.com, tells of a letter Walter sent to Edward in January 1916. He explained how he was stationed at Les Ciseaux, which was about 16 miles from the front line fighting.

'For the last three weeks my Battalion has been resting some miles distant from the firing line, but we are now going up to the trenches for a month or so. Afterwards we shall begin to think about coming home on leave. It is a very monotonous life out here when one is supposed to be resting and most of the boys prefer the action of the trenches.'

Chapter 2

Walter Tull's footballing career

Whilst a resident of the Bonner Street children's home, Walter showed an aptitude for most sports, but especially for cricket and football, the latter of which he quite excelled at, and was usually the one boy who caught the eye. He represented his children's home on many occasions and his impressive performances brought him to the attention of both amateur and professional football clubs.

In October 1908, a local amateur side, Clapton Football Club, which had been formed in 1878, was the first club to offer him a trial. He accepted and passed with flying colours and it wasn't long before he was a regular in the first team. By the end of the 1908 – 1909 season Clapton had become a very prominent club, winning not one, but three much respected competitions in the amateur ranks. They began their hat trick of wins with the prestigious FA Amateur Challenge Cup, which they won 6-0, by beating Easton United from the Northern League, regaining the trophy which they had won two years earlier in 1907 when they had beaten Stockton by the more respectable margin for the losers of 2-1. They also won the London Senior Cup in 1909 as well as the London County Amateur Cup. It was a remarkable season by anyone's standards and Walter Tull more than played his part in winning all three of those trophies.

As an amateur Walter did not get paid for playing football, so he needed a job. He needed to acquire a skill that could earn him a living for the long term, and decided to become a printer. He began his apprenticeship and training in 1905 in the workshops of the Bonner Road Children's Home, but it was always going to be a case of when, rather than if, he would become a professional footballer. He had been at Clapton for less than a year when Tottenham Hotspur acquired his signature.

Walter Tull first scored for Tottenham in a friendly match on 29 April 1909, at the end of the 1908 – 1909 season, when they beat Clapton Orient 3-2 in an away fixture. Walter scored two of the goals, Curtis being the other scorer. The beginning of the 1909 – 1910 season saw an incredible fourteen new faces arriving at White Hart Lane. Besides Walter Tull, the others were: D. Brown, D.H. Clark, J. Curtis, W. Harris, B. Ives, J.J. Laydon, P. McConnor, H. Middlemiss, C.H. Turrell, F. Wilkes, E. Bulling, P. Humphreys, and F. Drabble. After having impressed in trial matches for Tottenham's A-team and their reserves, he was invited to join them on their 1909 tour of Argentina.

The Argentine Football Association had invited Tottenham, along with Everton Football Club, who the previous season had finished runners up in the First Division, to come and play a couple of exhibition matches against each other, as well as playing games with some local sides. Walter Tull signed for Tottenham on 20 July 1909. The maximum wage a footballer could earn in those days was capped at £4 a week, which was a more than reasonable sum of money for the day. With no luxury air travel available then, the journey to Argentina had to be undertaken by ship and took three weeks rather than just a matter of hours as it would do today. The players had to undergo daily training on the ship's deck to ensure they maintained their levels of fitness.

The tour nearly didn't happen for Tottenham, as they got stuck in heavy traffic whilst they were crossing London. By the time they arrived at Waterloo Railway station, to catch their connecting train to Southampton, it had already left. They eventually managed to catch a later train, but by the time they arrived on the south coast, the ship they were due to board, the Royal Mail Steam Ship *Uraguaya*, had already sailed. Rather than lose out on the pre-season trip and simply give in to the situation in which they found themselves, the thirteen players and club officials quickly hired a nearby tug boat and climbed on board. After following the *Uraguaya* along the River Solent a short way, the vessel slowed and stopped, allowing the Tottenham party to transfer across, to the amusement and entertainment of the ship's other passengers who had managed to get on board in the more conventional manner at Southampton.

The journey took three weeks to complete, after the *Uraguaya* had made scheduled stops at the port of Cherbourg in France, to take on mail and other passengers. From there it was on to Vigo in Portugal where, after a brief stop, the vessel sailed along the Portuguese coastline, before arriving in Lisbon about 8.30am, where it remained until 6am the following morning. This allowed plenty of time for sightseeing, including the botanical gardens and the Black Horse Square, which had become famous as the site where Portugal's King Carlos had been assassinated. The afternoon was spent relaxing at the prestigious Café Royal. The vessel then carried on to the Portuguese island of Madeira, where there was a further stop with time for a relaxing stroll, sightseeing and a visit to the Cathedral of Our Lady of the Assumption, in the city of Funchal. The next port of call was at St Vincent in the Cape Verde Islands, for a stop of only a few hours, but whilst at anchor, all of the *Uraguaya's* passengers and crew were treated to an exhibition of high diving and copper diving, from the side of the ship's deck.

As the ship made its way across the Atlantic Ocean, en route to South America, celebrations were arranged in the shape of a fancy dress ball, to commemorate the national day of the independence of Argentina, which took place on 25 May. The Tottenham players had a choice of different costumes but what Walter wore is not recorded. The party atmosphere carried on throughout the day and on into the early hours of the following morning. The first stop in South America was on the far north-east corner of Brazil in Pernambuca, but it was only a short stay to collect more provisions before the vessel continued on its way, arriving in Rio de Janeiro at 7pm on the evening of Sunday 30 May, where it stayed at anchor until 6pm the following evening. There was quite a relaxed mood with plenty of time for the Tottenham party to do some sightseeing. Once they had tired themselves out with all the walking, they then had time to relax in fine establishments such as the Grand White Hotel, sipping ice cold drinks or perhaps even a cup of tea.

The *Uraguaya* left Rio de Janeiro at 6pm on the evening of 30 June and set out on the final leg of the cruise, reaching its final destination at Santos on the south-east coast of Brazil, at 8am on Tuesday 1 June, to be met by representatives of the Argentina Football Association, along with members of the Press.

The Tottenham touring party only consisted of thirteen players. There were: Boreham, Conquet, Wilkes, Bull, D. Steel, McFarlane, Curtis, Minter, Tull, Clarke, McConner, Morris and Middlemiss.

The first game of the tour took place at the Sociedad Sportiva in Palermo on 6 June 1909, with Tottenham playing against Everton, in what was an historic occasion, as the match was the first time that two professional teams had played each other throughout Latin America. The Tottenham team for the first match of the tour was; J. Boreham, F. Wilkes, E. Conquet, S. MacFarlane, D. Steel, W. Bull, M. Middlemiss, D. Clark, W. Tull, J. Minter and W. Curtis.

This was of course long before substitutes were allowed. The first use of them in the Football League took place on Saturday, 21 August 1965, when Keith Peacock of Charlton Athletic Football Club came on as a substitute, just eleven minutes into their away game with Bolton Wanderers, when Charlton's goalkeeper, Mike Rose, was injured. Later the same afternoon, Bobby Knox became the first substitute to score a goal when he scored for Barrow against Wrexham.

Both teams were introduced to the President of Argentina, Jose Maria Cornelio Figueroa Alcorta, members of his government and their families, not as is now the tradition, before the game begins, but at half time. The crowd of only 8,000 were rewarded with an entertaining game of football by the two English sides. The result of that first match was a 2-2 draw, with the Tottenham goals coming from Walter Tull and his striking partner, M. Middlemiss, with Balmer and Freeman replying for Everton.

There was no time to do much in the way of sightseeing for the Tottenham party, as four days after the game against Everton, they were in Montevideo, Uruguay, playing a match against a representative side from the Uruguayan League at the Central Park stadium. The game went the way that it would have been expected to, with Tottenham winning the match in convincing fashion by a score line of 8-0. The difference between a full time professional team playing against an amateur part-time side was clearly evident, both in the levels of physical fitness and the playing abilities of the individual players.

The man of the match for Tottenham that day was undoubtedly M. Middlemiss, who scored a hat trick, most probably one of the easier ones he had scored throughout his career. The other scorers being McConnor, Minter, D. Steel, and two goals by D. Clark.

The visit to Montevideo was only a brief one, as the Tottenham team had to be back in Palermo for a game against Argentina, at the Sociedad Sportiva stadium, which took place on 13 June 1909, in front of a passionate home crowd of over 14,000 spectators. The tourists again ran out winners, but this time only by the marginal score line of 1-0. McConnor scored the only goal of the game. An interesting footnote about this game was that of the Argentina team four had the surname Brown, another with the name Browne, one was Jacobs, one Watson and another was called Hutton.

With time being of the essence on the tour schedule, the games came around thick and fast, with Tottenham's next match taking place on 16 June in Palermo, once again at the Sociedad Sportiva stadium, but this time in front of a crowd of only 4,000 spectators. The opposition on this occasion were Liga Argentina, a representative team. Tottenham won 4-1 but reports of the match suggest that the score line could have been a much bigger one for the visitors, but a combination of poor finishing and good defending limited the score. It was one of those games where the final score did not reflect the true dominance Tottenham had throughout the match. Once again, most of the Argentinians had British sounding surnames.

The Tottenham team for this match were, J. Boreham, F. Wilkes, E. Coquet, S. MacFarlane, D. Steel, Morris, M. Middlemiss, D. Clark, W. Tull, J. Minter, and W. Curtis. Spurs scorers that day were Morris, who scored after only two minutes, Minter, Clark and MacFarlane. J. G. Brown replied for Liga Argentina, with a penalty in the twenty-seventh minute. The next match for Tottenham took place on 19 June and was the second occasion on the tour where they came up against Everton. This time the score wasn't such a flattering one for them, as they were soundly beaten 4-0 by an almost rampant Everton side. B. Freeman, scored a hat trick, his first two goals coming in the eleventh and twenty-seventh minutes. His third, which he tucked away from the penalty spot, was dispatched in the fifty-fourth minute. The scorer of the fourth Everton goal was H. Lacey.

Then it was off to Rosario for their next game at the Argentino stadium, where they played local side Liga Rosarina and soundly beat them 9-0. They were 3-0 up by half time, including an own goal by J. Diaz in the sixth minute. By the end of the match Tottenham had added a further six goals to their tally. The other goals came from Minter, who went crazy, claiming a total of five goals, MacFarlane, Middlemiss and Morris.

The last game of the tour took place on 24 June 1909 against Alumni at the Sociedad Sportiva stadium, a game which Tottenham won 5-0. W. Curtis opened the scoring after only five minutes. S. MacFarlane added a second in the fourteenth minute, Morris scored a third goal in the seventeenth minute, and J. Minter added the final two, his first coming in the twenty-fifth minute and the second in the eighty-eighth minute.

The Spurs team in that final game was, J. Boreham, F. Wilkes, E. Coquet, Morris, D. Steel, W. Bull, M. Middlemiss, S. MacFarlane, W. Tull, J. Minter, and W. Curtis.

By the end of the tour Tottenham had played seven games in the space of only eighteen days. They had won five of them, drawn one and lost one. Walter Tull had played in five of the games and scored one goal, but had suitably impressed with his overall play to warrant becoming a member of their first team squad for the forthcoming 1909/1910 season. It must have been an amazing tour, not only from a footballing sense, but experiencing different cultures, seeing so many beautiful sites and tasting different foods to what they were used to back home in England.

Despite the colour of Walter's skin, he explained in a letter sent home to his brother, Edward, how he had suffered from sunstroke during the tour, so hot were some of the temperatures which they experienced. This had led to his being ill for several days, which might explain why he had not played in two of the matches. The day after their last match of the tour, Friday, 25 June 1909, saw the Tottenham players and management board the Royal Mail Steamship *Asturias* in preparation for the home-ward journey, but because of a low tide and thick fog, the vessel didn't leave until Sunday 27 June. It was a slow steady journey, especially as the vessel made its way around the Brazilian and South American coastline, with as many stops as there had been on the outward bound journey from Southampton. Charles Roberts, the Tottenham Chairman at the time, wrote:

> 'On our way home we were anxious that the boys should see Brazil, a chance that they may never again have, we did Santos running up to San Paolo by rail, Rio de Janeiro, where we did the granite hills of Corcovado and Tijuca, perhaps the most beautiful spots under the sun. Also Madeira, where we mounted the hills and tobogganed down the cobbles, taking wine at the noted half way house.'

The journey back across the Atlantic Ocean took eight days, so vast is that particular expanse of water, before the ship reached Maderia. On 9 July, it was the anniversary of the Constitution of the Argentine Republic, so accordingly celebrations were held on board, which included singing and dancing along with a fancy dress competition. Third prize in this spectacle went to the Tottenham pair of Frederick Wilkes and Walter Tull, who were dressed up as Robinson Crusoe and Man Friday, two characters from Daniel Defoe's 1719 novel, *Robinson Crusoe*.

The nine weeks away on the tour of Argentina had certainly enabled Walter to form close bonds with his new team mates, who saw him for the skilful footballer and pleasant individual that he was. At the beginning of the 1914 – 1915 season Tottenham, having impressed their hosts during their tour to South America in 1909, were invited to tour Brazil, but they declined the invitation, possibly because the likelihood of war at that time.

The information about Tottenham's tour of Argentina in 1909, in the main came from, and with the permission of, Keith Harrison's blog, 'Hotspur Towers – Spurs in South America'.

During the First World War the *Asturias* was commandeered by the Admiralty, and turned in to a hospital ship, used mainly in such places as Salonika, Gallipoli and Egypt, from where she returned wounded British and other Allied soldiers back to the United Kingdom. She had sufficient berths to cater for 896 patients, although on one occasion she had on board a staggering total of 2,400 sick and wounded men, being transported back home. Luck was certainly on *Asturias's* side when on 1 February 1915 she was struck by a torpedo fired by a German submarine. Fortunately, it failed to explode. The German Government later admitted the attack, but claimed the U-boat which had fired the torpedo had done so mistakenly and once they had realised their mistake, they broke off the engagement.

The British author and poet John Ronald Reuel Tolkien, better known by his pen name of J.R.R. Tolkien, who served as a lieutenant in the Lancashire Fusiliers during the Battle of the Somme in 1916, was invalided back to the UK on board the *Asturias* on 8 November 1916, after being diagnosed with trench fever. He recollects there being salt baths on board.

On 20 March 1917, after having just unloaded 1,000 wounded men at Avonmouth, she began making her way to Southampton with the remainder, when she was torpedoed by the German submarine, *UC-66*. The captain of the stricken vessel managed to beach his ship near Bolt Head, in Devon. Despite thirty-one men losing their lives and twelve more being reported missing, this valiant act undoubtedly saved the lives of many of those still on board, especially as many were bed ridden and could not move due to the extent of their wounds.

The *Asturias* was salvaged and used as a floating ammunition ship anchored off Plymouth for two years. The Royal Mail Line bought the damaged ship from the government in 1920 and repaired and once again refitted her as a cruise liner, renaming her the *Arcadian*, sailing her on routes in the Mediterranean and the West Indies. She saw service all the way through to 1933 when she was scrapped.

Walter had been returned to England on board such a ship when he fell sick during the early years of the war, so he more than most would have appreciated the need for such vessels, nearly all of which had been ocean-going passenger liners before the outbreak of the war.

Becoming a professional footballer was the realisation of his childhood ambition. In reaching the professional ranks, he became only the third black man to do so in the United Kingdom, behind Arthur Wharton and Andrew Watson, although the latter played for Queen's Park, which was an amateur club. At 5ft 8in he wasn't a particularly tall man, but he had the strength, speed and ability to more than justify his selection in either midfield or as an out and out centre forward. He was still only 21 years of age when he made his Tottenham debut, on 11 September 1909 in front of a crowd estimated at 40,000 at White Hart Lane, against Manchester United. The match ended in a 2-2 draw, and although Walter didn't score either of the two Spurs goals, he was fouled for one of them which led to a penalty, from which they scored. The game was also notable as being Tottenham's first home match in the First Division of the Football League, as well as marking the opening of the ground's Old West Stand. The team that day was Boreham in goal, Coquet, Wilkes, Morris, D. Steel, Darnell, Curtis, Minter, Tull, R. Steel, Middlemiss.

Life in the First Division did not get off to an auspicious start for Tottenham. Their first two fixtures of the season had been away matches at Sunderland and Everton, both of which had ended in defeats, whilst Manchester United had won all of their first three matches. United took an early lead with Tottenham equalising from the penalty spot after Walter Tull was fouled by United's defender, Roberts. At half time the visitors held a 2-1 lead. Tottenham were awarded another penalty mid-way through the second half, with the spot kick being dispatched with great aplomb by R. Steele, his second of the match. Some reports of the match which appeared in the newspapers prefixed Walter's name with what would be a totally unacceptable terminology today, the word 'Darkie,' but which wasn't used in a negative or a derogatory manner at the time. Because of his performance that day against Manchester United, he very quickly became a favourite with the Tottenham Hotspurs fans.

Walter Tull scored his first goal for Tottenham in the Football League in their second game of the season in an away fixture at Bradford City, the week after his debut against Manchester United. Unfortunately, it was a game which they lost by the embarrassing score line of 5-1 in front of a crowd of 25,000 people. The home fixture against Bradford early the following year, ended in a 0-0 draw, allowing Tottenham to recover some credibility.

Tottenham only had to wait a short while for their first home victory of the season, when in their very next match, their fifth of the season, they beat Sheffield Wednesday, by a 3-0 score line, with goals coming from D. Steel, Curtis and Minter.

On 2 October 1909 during an away match at Bristol City, Walter was the target of some pretty bad racial abuse from a section of the home supporters, amongst a crowd of some 20,000 people, which was reported on in many of the national newspapers. For some reason, lost deep in the archives of history, Tottenham took what appears to be the somewhat strange decision to drop Walter to their reserve team soon afterwards. The club's management had obviously, in some way or another, been surprised by this incident and decided to move Walter to the reserves. During the rest of his time at Tottenham, he only made three more appearances for their first team. This was a sad decision, not only because of the circumstances in which it was made, but because it prevented the British public from seeing just how good a footballing talent Walter actually was.

Two games after the away match at Bristol City, where Walter had received some terrible racial abuse from a section of the Bristol City fans, he lost his place in the first team and was replaced by Percy Humphreys, who had been purchased from London neighbours Chelsea, and who went on to score eighteen goals in only twenty-four games, one more than Middlemiss who scored seventeen goals, and only three less than the twenty-one goals that top scorer Billy Minter managed to net. The latter went on to play for Tottenham for eighteen years until 1926. In his 334 appearances for the club, he scored 101 goals in all competitions.

Like Walter, Minter also served in the Army during the war. He returned to the club after he was demobilised and was made club captain. Having lost his automatic starting place in the side, he announced his retirement at the end of the 1919 – 1920 season, at the age of 32, but he didn't leave the club, staying on as a trainer, and on 28 February 1927 he was appointed first team manager, after Peter McWilliams resigned the position. Minter's first season was not a successful one and the club was relegated from Division One with a total of thirty-eight points. The seven teams that finished above them all amassed thirty-nine points, just one point more. If Tottenham had won just one of the nineteen games they had lost, or one of the eight games they had drawn, then they would have finished in twelfth position rather than twenty-first, and relegation, that's how close things were.

In their final six matches of the season, Tottenham lost four, won one, and drew one. They conceded fifteen goals and scored only eight in reply. It came down to their last game of the season, when they played Liverpool away at Anfield, a team they had already beaten 3-1 at home, earlier in the season. A draw would have left their fate determined on goal difference, a victory would have seen them safe, they lost the game 2-0, their fate sealed. The following season they finished tenth in Division Two, and the season after they finished twelfth. With his health failing, mainly due to his three seasons as manager, Minter resigned at the end of the 1929 – 1930 season, but remained at the club until his death on 21 May 1940 aged 52.

The only other competitive match Walter scored in for Tottenham during the 1909 – 1910 season was against Croydon Common at home on 11 October 1909 in the second round of the London Charity Cup, a match which Tottenham won 7-1. Once Walter had lost his place in the first team, no matter what the reason was for this happening, it was always going to be difficult for him to get it back, with three of his team mates scoring 56 goals between them, and all three of them having scored hat tricks.

In the last nine games of the season, Tottenham won four of their matches, drew three and lost only two of them. Humphreys scored in all of the four games that they won and two of the games which they drew. It could therefore easily be argued that dropping Walter Tull and replacing him with Percy Humphreys, went a long way to keeping Tottenham in the First Division of the Football League, although to be fair to Walter, it can now only be guessed at as to how many goals he might have scored if he had been played instead of Humphreys. Tottenham didn't have a particularly good season, but they did enough to remain in the league and were the best of the three London clubs, finishing in fifteenth place, with Arsenal finishing eighteenth and Chelsea, who finished in nineteenth, being relegated. Tottenham lost seventeen of their thirty-eight matches, ending up on thirty-two points.

Having only played seven first team games in the 1909 – 1910 season, the following year did not see Walter Tull fare any better, with him being selected to represent Tottenham's first team on just three occasions. He did, however, turn out twenty-seven times for the reserve team, where he scored ten goals. Walter's stats at Spurs show that he played for the first team on ten occasions, scoring just two goals.

During one of those reserve games between Tottenham and Northampton Town in February 1911, Walter scored a stunning goal after only eleven minutes of the game. He went on to score a hat trick in a 7-1 victory. Impressed with what they had seen, Northampton put in a bid for Walter and, with the deal completed, he signed for Northampton Town in October 1911 for what was reported to be a 'substantial fee' although the actual amount was never disclosed. It was a decision that he would not regret. He began living in lodgings at 39 Queen Street, Rushden, Northampton, along with one of his team mates, Eric Feltham Tomkins. The 1911 Census showed Eric as an 18-year-old teacher. The lady of the house was Miss Annie Williams.

Part of the Northampton Town deal included right back Charlie Brittain moving from Northampton Town to Tottenham Hotspur, where he played forty matches over the course of two seasons before moving on to Cardiff City, where he spent the remaining nine years of his career, retiring in 1922 aged 35.

At the time of the transfer Northampton Town were managed by the young and forward thinking Herbert Chapman, who had also played for the club during his own playing days and would go on to win the FA Cup and First Division League title with both Huddersfield Town and Arsenal as their managers. When Walter Tull signed for Northampton Town, Herbert Chapman, was only 31 years of age. Walter played more than one hundred first team matches for Northampton Town, before the outbreak of the war brought a premature end to his career as a professional footballer.

Tottenham Hotspur, or rather their ground, White Hart Lane, played an interesting part in the history of the First World War. When hostilities broke out, for some strange reason the government of the day decided to commandeer the club's football stadium. With all of the large buildings that would have suddenly been available to them under the legislation provided by the terms of the Defence of the Realm Act 1914, they somehow decided that their best and most viable option was White Hart Lane football ground. The reason why the government commandeered it was not, as one might think, so that it could used as a military barracks, a location where they could store armaments, a military hospital, or a mortuary, as part of the ground was used for during the Second World War, but to make gas masks. As a result of this governmental decision, Tottenham had to play their home games at the ground of their arch North London rivals, the Woolwich Arsenal.

Walter made three guest appearances for Fulham during the 1915 – 1916 season, before eventually signing for Glasgow Rangers in February 1917 whilst in Scotland on his officer training course, with the intention of playing for them after the war. His death the following year put paid to that becoming a reality. The main reason he chose to sign for Glasgow Rangers, was so that he could be close to his brother Edward, who had lived in the city since being adopted by the Warnock family in November 1900.

An article appeared in the *Northampton Mercury* newspaper dated Friday, 15 August 1919, about Northampton Town's prospects for the 1919 – 1920 season, with the aftermath of the First World War still not seeing all of the men having returned home. Professional football had been suspended throughout the war years, and the forthcoming campaign would be the first since the 1914 – 1915 season. There had been some football played in England throughout the war, but these games were in the main either friendlies or representative matches. After the war Northampton Town football club was missing a vast array of the players who had played for them before the war. Some like Walter Tull had been killed, whilst others were still in the Army waiting to be demobbed. One of the real issues for Northampton Town was the financial side of things, and it was immediately clear that for the club to once again become competitive it needed its fans to support the club by turning up to home matches to bring in much needed revenue. Although this did not necessarily mean that new players could be bought, it certainly allowed the club's management to maintain the playing strength of the team and to invest in some young players to be kept in reserve.

Nearly all the team from the 1914 – 1915 season who had left to go off to war, were re-engaged. Tom Thorpe was coming back as the goalkeeper, with Lloyd Davies returning at left back, although he had turned out for Millwall during the course of the 1918 – 1919 season. Eric Tomkins, who had also spent the previous season playing for Tottenham Hotspur, and who had also played representative matches for the Royal Air Force, returned. Jack Manning, Grendon and Emery, all signed professional contracts with the club. Whitworth, a young and impressive centre forward, who had spent the previous season knocking in goals for Crystal Palace, had signed, as had Freeman Rushton, a local top amateur player who, it was believed, would comfortably make it in the professional game.

One player they could not welcome back was Walter Tull. His death was seen as a massive loss to the club, a man who was equally effective playing in either midfield or in one of the three forward positions. Walter was not the only pre-war Northampton Town player to be killed during the war.

The newly assembled Northampton Town squad met up together for the first time on Saturday, 16 August 1919. Mr Alf Burrows was the team's manager. As a mark of respect to their former player, in 1999 Northampton Town Football Club unveiled a memorial to Walter outside the Sixfields Stadium, and the road leading up to it is now officially known as 'Walter Tull Way'.

Arthur Wharton

Walter was not the only black footballer of his generation, nor was he the first. Arthur Wharton had become the first non-white professional

footballer in England, twenty years before Walter Tull, when he joined
Rotherham Town. He was born in what is today Ghana, on 28 October
1865, to parents Henry and Annie Wharton. Annie was a member of the
Ghanaian royal family. Arthur arrived in England in 1882 when he was
19 years old to train as a Methodist Minister, but he had a change of
heart and decided that his desire to become a professional sportsman was
much stronger than his will to become a missionary. The question was,
which sport, as he was a proficient cyclist, runner, cricketer and footballer. Eventually he decided on football.

Arthur's professional career spanned thirteen years, during which
time he played for six different clubs, but he only played a total of thirteen league games during that time. During the 1885 – 1886 season,
when they won the Durham Challenge Cup, Arthur played one game for
Darlington football club, who had only been formed in 1883. The following season he signed as an amateur for the mighty Preston North End
football club who, in the inaugural season of the Football League (1888
– 1889), did not lose a single game winning the league and cup double. Sadly for Arthur, he took the decision to leave Preston in 1888 after
having played for them only twice, so that he could concentrate on his
running, hence missing out on being part of the 'Double' winning side.

In 1889 he returned to playing football and signed his first professional contract with Rotherham Town, where he remained for five years
until the end of the 1893 – 1894 season, despite not making one league
appearance for them. In the 1894 – 1895 season he signed for Sheffield
United who played in Division One of the Football League. He was the
understudy to the famous goalkeeper, William 'Fatty' Foulkes, and when
Arthur played his one league game of the season against Sunderland, he
became the first non-white professional footballer to play in the top flight
of the Football League.

In the two seasons between 1895 and 1897, Arthur played for Stalybridge
Rovers, during which time he made just four appearances. From there he
moved on to Ashton North End football club, which he played for until

the end of the 1898 – 1899 season when they went bankrupt and folded. By now he was 34 years of age. He then returned to Stalybridge Rovers for the next two seasons, only playing one league game in that time. It was here that he met a young Herbert Chapman, who would later become Walter Tull's manager at Northampton Town.

His final season was 1901 – 1902, during which time he made six league appearances and scored two goals for Stockport County in Division Two of the Football League, by which time he had already developed a drink problem.

In the previous eleven seasons, since he had turned professional in 1889, he had played for four clubs, but had only played a total of seven league matches. Besides being a goalkeeper he also played as a winger, and had scored one other league goal during his career for Stalybridge Rovers. After retiring as a professional footballer he went into the mining industry to earn a living at Edlington Colliery in Doncaster, South Yorkshire. He died in 1930 aged 65.

Andrew Watson

Andrew Watson is an extremely interesting character who pre-dates Arthur Wharton and comes with an amazing story that almost outdoes that of Walter Tull.

Andrew was born on 24 May 1856 in Demerara, in British Guiana, which had been a Dutch colony until 1815. He was the son of a wealthy Scottish sugar planter Peter Miller Watson and a local woman named Hannah Rose. He came to live in England in his early teens with his elder sister, Annetta and their father Peter and, when the latter passed away in London in 1869, he left both of his children a substantial sum of money. Andrew certainly moved around either intentionally or otherwise. He went to Heath Grammar School in Halifax, West Yorkshire, which had been founded in 1585. In 1871 he attended the King's College School in Wimbledon, which then was one of the very finest and most progressive in the country. One of the subjects taught at the school was science at a

time when it was taught at very few educational establishments throughout the land, deemed by many educators as unnecessary. It was also a
school which excelled at most sports of the day and encouraged its pupils
to participate in them. This was where Andrew first acquired his love for
the game.

In 1876 when he was 19 years old he attended the University of
Glasgow in his father's native Scotland, where he studied natural philos-
ophy, mathematics, engineering, and also continued to play his beloved
football. He dropped out of university after only one year and went into
partnership with Watson, Miller and Baird, who were in the wholesale
warehouse business in Glasgow.

Despite attending university and being in business, Andrew still
found time to play football, for both Maxwell and Parkgrove Football
Clubs, although the game in Scotland at the time still only had amateur status. The Scottish Football Association was founded in 1873 by
a group of eight amateur Scottish football clubs, including Queen's
Park which had been formed in 1867 and was based in Glasgow, but
wanted to keep the game on an amateur basis. It would be nearly
twenty years before the Scottish Football League began in 1890, but
Queen's Park elected not join until 1893, by which time the game in
Scotland was on a professional level.

Andrew had played for Parkgrove Football Club for six years between
1874 and 1880, and was then transferred to Scotland's most prestigious
club of the day, Queen's Park, where he would spend the next two years.
During this time he was also capped three times for the Scottish national
side. His first appearance for Scotland was in a game against England
which was played in London on 12 March 1881, making him the first
black man to play international football for any of the British nations or
Ireland. Andrew captained the side from left full back and Scotland won
6-1. A few days later Scotland played against Wales and won 5-1. His
third, and what would also turn out to be his final cap, was against England
in Glasgow on 11 March 1882, with Scotland once again winning the

match, this time by a score line of 5-1. Andrew would have undoubtedly gone on to represent Scotland on many future occasions, but later that year he moved London, where he began playing for the Swifts Football Club, based in Slough, Berkshire. This in effect ended his international career with Scotland because at the time the Scottish Football League had a policy of only picking players who were based in Scotland.

To put Andrew's achievement of being selected to play international football for Scotland in some kind of context, it is worth noting that the next black man to be selected to represent Scotland at football was Nigel Quashie in 2004 when he played against Estonia, meaning that there was a gap of 122 years between the first and second black man to have represented Scotland at football. Between 2004 and 2006 Nigel made a total of fourteen appearances for Scotland. Prior to this he had also represented England at both Under 21 and 'B' level.

Paul Wilson, who was Asian, having been born in Bangalore, India in 1950, to a Scottish father and a Dutch-Portuguese mother, was selected to play for Scotland at full international level in 1975 against Spain in Valencia, when he came on as a 75th minute substitute for his one and only full international cap. He retired from professional football at the age of only 29. He did subsequently win a further Scottish international cap at non-league, or what is also referred to as junior football.

Andrew spent two years playing with the Swifts football club, before transferring to the Corinthians football club in 1884, where he played for just one season, before he returned to Scotland and Queen's Park, where he stayed for two years until 1887. Later that year aged 31, he transferred to the Bootle Football Club on Merseyside, where he saw out his playing days, turning out for them until the end of the 1891 – 1892 season, when he retired aged 36. Bootle were an interesting club. They were known to offer wages and signing on fees, which allowed them to attract some really good players. There is no known record which shows if Andrew was one such player, but if he was, and even though Bootle were not a professional club, then he would have been, albeit technically, the first ever black professional footballer to have played anywhere throughout Great Britain, as Arthur Wharton didn't sign professional terms until 1889.

Andrew died in London of pneumonia in 1921 aged 65.

William Gibb Clarke

William Gibb Clarke, who was more commonly known as Billy or Willie, was a Scottish professional footballer who was born on 3 March 1878 in the small town of Mauchline in East Ayrshire. William's last season of playing was in 1911- 1912, by which time Walter Tull was playing with Northampton Town Football Club.

William was a speedy winger who played for a total of eight different teams, five of which – Benburb, Crown Athletic, Third Lanark, Arthurlie and East Stirlingshire – were all Scottish clubs, and Bristol Rovers, Aston Villa, Bradford City, Lincoln City and Croydon Common, in England.

Having joined Bristol Rovers on 23 August 1900, he was with them for just one season, 1900 – 1901, during which time he played for them on twenty-two occasions, scoring seven goals. On 18 May 1901 he was trans-ferred to Aston Villa, who at the time played their football in the old First Division of the Football League. William played a total of forty-three matches, scoring six goals during his four year spell at the club. His first goal for them made him the first non-white player to score a goal in the Football League.

He was transferred to Bradford City for the sum of £200 on 2 May 1905 and over the next four seasons he played ninety-two games for the club, scoring a total of sixteen goals. In 1905 he was part of the Bradford City team which won the Second Division Championship, and he was the player who scored Bradford City's first ever goal in the First Division.

On 18 September 1909 a remarkable occasion took place when Tottenham played Bradford City away at Valley Parade in the First Division. Bradford won the match 5-1 with Walter Tull scoring the Spurs goal. But that wasn't what made it remarkable. Not only did Walter Tull play for Tottenham that day, but William Clarke was playing for Bradford City, which was probably the first time that two non-white men had played professional football against each other and it was certainly a first for the First Division of the Football League.

In December 1909, aged 31, William signed for Lincoln City, where he remained for the next two seasons, playing thirty-five games and scoring just a solitary goal. In September 1911 William signed for his tenth and last club, Croydon Common. Despite being 33 years of age, he played for them a total of forty-three times, and scored seven goals.

Billy died in London in 1940 aged 62.

Edwin and John Cother

The Cother brothers, Edwin and John, played football for Watford Football Club in 1898. Edwin, the younger of the two, was born in Uxbridge in 1877 and was somewhat of a utility player, and not too shoddy when it came to the game of cricket either by all accounts, whilst John junior, who was also born in Uxbridge, in 1872, excelled as a fullback. Their father, John, was born in India, and their mother, Elizabeth, was born in High Wycombe, Buckinghamshire. The two young men were noticeably dark skinned and were referred to by a nickname which would be deemed politically incorrect and totally unacceptable by today's standards.

The 1901 Census recorded Edwin as being a general labourer, whilst ten years later, when he was still only 34 years of age, and living at 15 Neston Road, Watford, Hertfordshire, with his wife Alice and their three children, he was shown as a bricklayer. By the time of the 1911 Census, John, who by then was 39 years of age and also a labourer, was shown as living at the Watford Union Workhouse and Infirmary, which was situated at 60 Vicarage Road, Watford.

There were numerous newspaper articles concerning games played by Watford; the *Herts Advertiser* carried some in depth match reports. One in particular caught the eye from the newspaper's edition of Saturday, 2 November 1901, covering their game against Tottenham Hotspur, played the week before on 26 October, a game which was won by Tottenham by the rather embarrassing score line of 8-1. Part of the article read as follows.

> 'Eight goals to one is a score which requires a lot of explaining, but I must state that had it not been for the splendid defensive work on the part of Cother, Nidd and Waller, the score would have been almost double what it was. Cother was especially noticeable, for he was as good a back as there was on the field, or at least he played the best game of either of the four. Nidd greatly assisted him.'

John Walker

John Walker was born in 1878 in Leith, Scotland. He was black, played football for Heart of Midlothian and Lincoln City and was dead by the time he was 22 years of age. Other than these facts, not a lot is really known about his background with any certainty. His mother, Sarah, was born in the Scottish port town of Leith, and his father John, who in the 1881 Census, is shown as being a dock labourer, and is believed to have been born in the West Indies, which is recorded on the same census as 'India, West.'

The following article appeared in the edition of the *Dundee Courier* newspaper dated Tuesday, 7 August 1900.

> 'The death is announced of John Walker, the well-known coloured football player residing in Leith. He was better known as "Darkey" Walker and is believed to have been the only professional football player of colour in Scotland. Walker, on joining Leith Athletic three years ago, gave promise of developing into a class player, his tricky play and dashing runs establishing him a warm favourite. The Heart of Midlothian entered into negotiations for his transfer, which was effected for the sum of £50. After playing for the Hearts for a season, the Tyne-castle club gave Walker his papers, and at the beginning of last season he joined Lincoln City. He did not remain long with the English club, and returned home six months ago in ill health. Consumption was the cause of his death.'

The comment about him being the only professional football player of colour in Scotland was clearly forgetting the likes of Arthur Watson, who besides being black, had also played international football for Scotland on three occasions between 1881 and 1882. Walker only played three league matches for Hearts, and six for Lincoln City due in the main to his illness. His tragic death at such an early age brought to an abrupt end what would have no doubt been a glittering footballing career, one that was extinguished before it ever had the opportunity to fully flourish.

Frederick Corbett

Frederick Corbett was born in West Ham on 1 January 1881. He went on to become one of the few early black professional footballers, who in the 1899 – 1900 season, played for Thames Ironworks, where he was employed as a labourer. The following season he played for the same club, under their new name of West Ham United. In the 1901 – 1902 season, the same one that saw the Football League bring in a maximum wage of £4, Frederick Corbett, according to John Simpkin, from spartacus-education.com, scored a hat-trick against Wellingborough, making him one of the first, if not the first black men to score a hat trick in the Football League.

Over the following ten years he would play for four more clubs, Bristol City, Brentford, Gillingham, and Bristol Rovers, which he would sign for on three separate occasions. The 1911 Census shows Frederick living at 9 Woodborough Street, Stapleton Road, Bristol, where he was living, whilst playing for Bristol Rovers for the third time, along with his wife, Kate, and their two children, Winifred and Irene.

At the time of his death on 15 April 1924, he was 43 years of age.

Hassan Hegazi

Hassan Hegazi, who played football for Fulham in the Football League and Millwall and Dulwich Hamlet in the Southern League, was born in Cairo, Egypt on 14 September 1891. Phil Vasili describes in his book,

Colouring Over the White Line. The history of Black Footballers in Britain, how Hegazi only played one game for Fulham in a 3-1 win over Stockport County on 11 November 1911 during the 1911 – 1912 season, scoring one of the goals and making another. The following season he was transferred to Millwall where he also only played one match, before ending up at Dulwich. He also played in the annual 'varsity match for Cambridge University against Oxford, after becoming a student at St Catherine's College. Why it was that he ended up playing only one match for both Fulham and Millwall, is not known.

I do not suggest that the men I have mentioned above are a comprehensive list of every single black, Indian and Asian footballer, who played the game at the top level in English or Scotland. Those I have mentioned above are purely intended to provide a balance and perspective in relation to the achievements realised by Water Tull.

Chapter Three

Walter Tull's Military Service

At the outbreak of the war, and despite being a professional foot-baller at the time, Walter Tull volunteered and enlisted into the newly formed 17th (Football) Battalion, Middlesex Regiment, on 21 December 1914, and was allocated the service number of 55. Within two months he had been promoted to the rank of lance corporal, followed four months later with a further promotion to lance sergeant in June 1915.

Maybe it had been whilst reading his local newspaper, the *Northampton Mercury*, that Walter had been moved to enlist in the Army and go and do his bit. In those early months of the war, the paper was full of reports of acts of 'derring do', of men being wounded, killed, missing in action, bravery awards, and letters sent home from the front to worried friends and relatives.

The men from Northamptonshire didn't just join their local regiment, or all gravitate towards the Army to undertake their military service, they took up arms with many different agencies. In the first five months of the war the Commonwealth War Graves Commission records that a total of 381 men of the Northamptonshire Regiment were killed. This saw men of all ranks and all standings in society lose their lives in their pursuance of the common cause of defeating Germany. In the newspaper's edition dated Friday, 2 October 1914 under the heading 'Stirring Letters' was this:

> *'This week's list of casualties, together with the letters, which many of the wounded men have written, indicate that the Northamptonshires have been in the thick of the fighting. That the Regiment has*

conducted itself in a manner worthy of the great records behind it is certain, and Northamptonshire has reason to be proud of the part they are playing in the campaign.'

Walter Tull would have no doubt read about many men whom he didn't know, but who knew him, or at least knew who he was and would have seen him playing for Northampton Town Football Club. The men would have cheered him on whilst standing on the terraces at Sixfields stadium, no matter what the weather, through the good times and the not so good times. They would have clapped, cheered and rejoiced when he scored and been frustrated when he had missed a chance to score, but he was one of them, doing his best for their common cause, which was their beloved Northampton Town Football Club.

The colour of his skin didn't matter to them; all they cared about was that every time he pulled on the shirt and played for Northampton, he gave of his best for the good of the team. With the outbreak of the war, it was his turn to support them and become one of their number in the fight against another common cause, which on this occasion was the might of the Imperial German Army and the Kaiser's desire to beat Britain and her Allies into submission and rule over the rest of Europe.

One particular story concerned a young Northampton man who had no doubt watched Walter Tull play football from the terraces, as a supporter of his home town. It was representative of all the other letters and articles that were covered in that particular edition of the newspaper. The man in question was a Gunner (35387) Arthur William Thompson of the 48th Heavy Battery, Royal Garrison Artillery, who was, according to the War Office, killed in action on 13 September 1914, although the Commonwealth War Graves Commission website, records his death as a day later on 14 September. Gunner Thompson was a married man and the details of his death were recorded in a letter sent to his widow, received by her on Friday, 2 October 1914, and which unusually had been sent by the mother of the officer to whom Thompson had acted as servant. The writing of such letters was usually the responsibility of the dead man's platoon lieutenant. The woman who wrote the letter gives the date of Thompson's death as being 14 September 1914. She quotes her son as saying that Thompson *'died bravely at his post for his country, and our battery has been congratulated by the generals. We were told we saved the situation. You will be proud to feel that your husband had a share in this grand deed.'*

Gunner Thompson was well known in Northampton. By all accounts he was quite a young man, who was also very popular. At the time of his death, Arthur's parents Mr and Mrs William J. Thompson, lived at 51 Grafton Street, Northampton, but by the end of the war they had moved to 42 Monks Pond Street, in the town. He was described in the newspaper article as being 'a fine specimen of British manhood'.

The British Army believed that it was good practice to place men in battalions with other men from a similar work background, or who had a similar interest, such as the three Post Office Rifles (8th) Battalions of the London Regiment, or in the same regiment, who were mainly drawn from public schools and universities. The reason behind this particular approach was the belief by senior military officers that it helped produce better soldiers and a strong camaraderie between the men.

In 1914 England, black people were not treated as equals by the majority of white people, and some senior officers in the British Army held the belief that black people were not as intelligent and were concerned that white soldiers would not wish to fight alongside black soldiers, let alone be led by them. But regardless of the colour of Walter's skin, he was a very well known individual due to his exploits as a professional footballer, so it is more than likely that he was treated very differently from an ordinary black man would have been in the Army, by both senior officers and men from the other ranks.

After having completed his initial training, he first arrived in France in December 1915, right in the middle of a particularly cold winter, with most of his time being spent in the uncomfortable surroundings of newly dug trenches. It quickly became evident that Walter Tull was an exceptional man and had the leadership qualities required to become an officer.

By May 1916, Walter, who had already proved himself as a brave and competent soldier, was invalided back to England on board HM Hospital Ship, *Saint Denis*, suffering with 'acute mania'. The phrase 'shell shock' had not yet been coined, which for some men could be an extremely debilitating condition. The *Saint Denis* had originally been launched on 25 August 1908 and was named the SS *Munich* working as a passenger ferry for the Great Eastern Railway Company, with a route between Harwich and the Hook of Holland. After the outbreak of the war she was commandeered by the Admiralty on 12 October 1914, and turned into a hospital ship. Her medical staff consisted of four doctors/officers, six nurses and twenty-eight orderlies. The officers and orderlies would have been men from the Royal Army Medical Corps. The *Saint Denis* continued in this capacity until 18 October 1919, and had the capacity to accommodate fourteen officers with enough cots and berths to carry a total of 217 men from the other ranks.

Initially Walter was admitted to a nearby field hospital in France, before being sent back to England for further treatment. An interesting aside to this was a brief newspaper report dated Friday, 18 August 1916, which said: *'Walter Tull, the Cobblers' half back, who is in the Players Battalion, has been in hospital for three months with pneumonia, but is now convalescent.'*

Although reports showed that he was sent home from the war suffering from what in essence was 'shell shock', the edition of the *Northampton Mercury* newspaper dated Friday, 18 August 1916, clearly showed he had been treated for the effects of pneumonia and was convalescing.

During the course of the war Walter saw action in six battles: the Battle of the Ancre (November 1916), part of the first Battle of the Somme; the Battle of Messines (June 1917); Third Ypres (also known as the Battle of Passchendaele (July – November 1917); the Second Battle of the Somme and the First Battle of Bapaume (both in March 1918 during the German Spring Offensive).

Two of Walter's cousins, George Thomas Palmer and Stephen John Alexander Palmer, were both killed during the First World War. Their father, John Palmer, who was the brother of Walter's mother Alice, also had three other sons who served during the war and survived: William John Palmer, Edwin George Palmer and Walter Henry Palmer. Another of Walter's cousins, Charles Richard D. Palmer, the son of another of Alice's brother, Richard, was also killed.

Private George Thomas Palmer (G/5181) served in the 8th Battalion, The Buffs. He was killed in action during the Battle of the Somme on 19 August 1916. George was Walter's cousin, and like him his body was never recovered and he has no known grave. His name is commemorated on the Thiepval Memorial, which is situated in the Somme region of France.

Stephen John Alexander Palmer had originally enlisted at Dover into the 1st Battalion, The Buffs (East Kent Regiment) as Private 10174, but later in the war transferred to the Queen's (Royal West Surrey Regiment) where he eventually became a Lance Serjeant (S/7023) in the 7th Battalion. At only 20 years of age he was also killed in action, on 16 July 1917. Like George and Walter, Stephen has no known grave and is commemorated on the Menin Gate Memorial, Ypres.

In death Stephen's luck had most definitely run out, although good fortune had been on his side when on a previous occasion he had been shot in the chest by a German bullet, but other than having the wind knocked out of him and few bruises, he miraculously survived. The bullet passed through his tobacco tin which he kept in the breast pocket of his tunic, but it failed to pierce a metal OXO tin which was immediately behind the tobacco tin, in the same pocket.

The War Diaries of the 7th Battalion, the Queen's (Royal West Surrey Regiment) show that they were in front line trenches at Zillebeke in Belgium from 14 July 1917 and had been heavily shelled by German artillery, which included the deployment of gas shells. Throughout the day on 15 July it had been very quiet, but at 10pm that evening the Germans opened up with a heavy artillery bombardment, which targeted the front line trenches defended by men from the 7th Battalion. By the time the attack was over, four men from the other ranks had been killed whilst another four had been wounded. Second Lieutenant C.N. de Trafford was conveyed to hospital, but the diaries did not record details of his injuries or wounds.

The entry for 16 July records that Second Lieutenant Hoxey had been granted special leave to England, whilst Second Lieutenant Esdon had been transferred to the Second Corps School as an instructor. It also shows once again that the front line trenches where men from the 7th Battalion were stationed were heavily shelled by German artillery, which resulted in seven men from the other ranks being killed and another twelve wounded. Stephen Palmer was one of those killed.

There were three other brothers serving in the Army. **Private William John Palmer** served with the Royal Garrison Artillery and was awarded the Distinguished Conduct Medal for bravery. **Private Edwin George Palmer,** 1st Battalion, The Buffs, was the eldest of the brothers who had been in the Army long before the First World War. The 1901 Census records him as being 24 years of age stationed at the Army Barracks in Northgate, Canterbury, although by the 1911 Census, he is back living at home at 22 Lansdowne Cottages, Union Road, Dover and working as a cowman. He may have joined the Army when he was 18 years of age in 1895 and enlisted for a period of twelve years, the usual period of time that men joined the Army for. This was split into serving for five years with the Colours and a further seven years in the Army Reserve. This would have taken Edwin through to 1907, when it appears that he left the Army and reverted to civilian life, and then simply re-joined once the First World War began. **Private Walter Henry Palmer,** who was the second youngest of the brothers, was later with the 8th Battalion, The Buffs, but at the outbreak of the war he was still only 15 years of age. He survived the war.

Charles Richard D. Palmer was a Chief Stoker in the Royal Navy (299617) when he was killed in action on 27 April 1916, when the ship he was serving on, HMS *Russell*, a Duncan-class pre-dreadnought battleship, struck two mines which had been laid by the German submarine, *U-73*. This caused an explosion and a fire to break out on the *Russell*. At the time of the sinking the vessel was steaming off Malta.

Initially 105 men were killed, but seven officers and two ratings died of their injuries on Friday, 28 April 1916, with a further two ratings dying on 29 April, another died on 11 May and one more on 23 May. Of those men who were killed in the sinking of the *Russell*, the bodies of only eleven of them were recovered from the sea, all of whom were buried at the Capuccini Naval Cemetery in Malta.

One of those who survived the sinking was Lieutenant Commander John H.D. Cunningham. He would later go on to become First Sea Lord, head of the Royal Navy.

U-73, the German submarine ultimately responsible for sending HMS *Russell* to a watery grave had, by the end of the war, sunk twenty-one British and Allied vessels and damaged three others. Only three of the vessels sunk were warships, seventeen were merchant vessels and one was a hospital ship. On 23 November 1916, a mine which had been laid by *U-73* was struck by HM Hospital Ship *Braemar Castle* whilst at sea in the Mykoni Channel in the Aegean Sea, with the loss of four lives. Two days before this another mine laid by *U-73* was responsible for the sinking of HM Hospital Ship *Britannic*.

The *Britannic* was the third of the White Star Line's Olympic Class vessels and was the sister ship to both the RMS *Olympic* and RMS *Titanic*. At 48,158 gross tons, she was also the largest vessel to be sunk during the First World War. She was launched on 26 February 1914 but was then requisitioned by the Admiralty on 13 November 1915 and refitted as a Hospital Ship, beginning her service in that capacity on 23 December 1915. Her captain was Charles Alfred Bartlett, who had been in the Royal Naval Reserve since 1893. She struck a mine on 21 November 1916 whilst sailing in the Kea Channel off the Greek island of Kea on 21 November 1916, and sank in under an hour. Of the 1,065 patients, staff and crew on board, 1,035 survived.

Remarkably, Walter Tull had recovered sufficiently within just three months, and was sent back to his unit, which by now had become the 23rd (2nd Football) Battalion of the Middlesex Regiment, which was still in France, arriving there on 20 September 1916. He was then promoted to the rank of serjeant before taking part in the Battle of Le Transloy, one of the actions of the Battle of the Somme, on 29 October 1916.

During the subsequent fighting, the Middlesex Regiment lost a total of 3,155 men killed. Out of Walter's section of some 400 men, only 79 remained alive. Having survived the fighting on the Somme, he was given leave and made it home to England on 26 December 1916, just in time to join in with the festive celebrations.

Lieutenant Colonel Haig-Brown, Walter's commanding officer, and one of the men who would end up dying on the same day as him, was suitably impressed by the young man under his command and saw in him what he recognised as leadership qualities. He had no qualms about recommending him for a place on a forthcoming officers' training course taking place at Gailes in Ayrshire, Scotland, which was one of the twenty-five Officer Training Battalions located around the British Isles.

As the war carried on much longer than had been anticipated, so it was that more and more officers were required to replace those who were being killed. With the need for more officers a new system was put in place in February 1916, to identify men from the ranks who had leadership potential. But before these men could be awarded temporary commissions they had to fulfil a set criteria; they had to be over 18 and a half years of age, have either been part of an officer cadet section, or served in the ranks. The course lasted for four and a half months and could cater for up to 400 men at a time, which by May 1917 had risen to 600. By the end of the war over 73,000 men had been awarded commissions in this way.

The course was not surprisingly very intense and consisted of many different aspects of military life, including tactics, command, leadership, map reading, grenade throwing, tactical use of machine guns, the use of pigeons to send messages and how to build and maintain trenches. Candidates had to be able to remain calm in the face of adversity, even if they had been overcome with fear, they could not show this to their men, and they had to be able to think on their feet and be adaptable in any given situation.

After successfully completing his course, Walter passed out as Second Lieutenant Walter Tull on 29 May 1917, but he did not return to France for a further three months, where he once again served with the Middlesex Regiment. The fact that Walter had been recommended for the course was amazing enough in itself, but for him to be accepted and subsequently pass, without any obvious opposition was a ground-breaking achievement. There were other black officers in the British Army at the time, but they did not serve in infantry units and as such were not in command of white soldiers.

Walter's first taste of action and leading his men into a baptism of fire, came at the Battle of Passchendaele, also known as the Third Battle of Ypres. Although the campaign commenced on 31 July 1917, the declining weather had already arrived before Walter and his men became involved. It was wet and cold, with the front line a series of waterlogged shell holes in a morass of liquid mud. Passchendaele became synonymous with the carnage and suffering of the First World War.

Although the battle was seen as an Allied victory, after more than three months of fighting only an estimated five miles of land had been captured from the Germans, with casualties that have been economically estimated in the region of 250,000. Of these, 1,170 men from the Middlesex Regiment were either killed in action or subsequently died of their wounds, 72 of whom were members of Walter's 23rd Battalion.

Soon after the end of the battle in November 1917, Walter's battalion was sent to northern Italy, to help in the fight against both Austrian and German forces, along the River Piave, north-west of Treviso. The battalion arrived on 21 November. Whilst there Walter volunteered on more than one occasion to cross over the river Piave, under cover of darkness, where elements of the German Army were based. These dangerous night-time sorties involved both evidence gathering and carrying out an attack. On both occasions, not only did Walter return unscathed, but he did so without incurring a single casualty amongst his men, feats which greatly impressed his commanding officer, Major General (later Sir) Sydney Lawford, who mentioned him in despatches, and recommended him for the award of the Military Cross, which he never received.

Sydney Lawford warrants a mention at this junction. His full name was Sydney Turing Barlow Lawford, and he finished the war as Lieutenant Colonel Sir Sydney Turing Barlow Lawton, having received his knighthood in the field in 1918. Like Walter Tull, he was a Kent man, born in Tunbridge Wells on 16 November 1865. He first married when he was 28 years of age on 28 September 1893, to Lilian Maud Cass, who died on 26 November 1900, by which time he was already an officer in the British Army, serving as a captain during the Second Boer War in South Africa.

He married for a second time, this time to Muriel Williams, on 20 May 1914, just three months before the outbreak of the First World War. He had a nickname, not one that was mentioned to his face, of 'Swanky Syd', supposedly because of his penchant for wearing his full dress uniform, including all of his medals, on every possible occasion. After the war he remained in the Army, and during the early 1920s was sent out to India, having been promoted to the rank of lieutenant general. Whilst serving in India, and still married to his second wife Muriel, he fell in love with the wife of one of the officers under his command, May Somerville Aylen. Colonel Aylen, on hearing of the scandal, as such behaviour most definitely was at the time, divorced his wife over the affair. The actions of Sydney Lawton would not have been received well in polite society of the day, or the officer class in general. It would have been seen as appalling behaviour, and certainly not the kind expected of such a high-ranking officer of the British Army.

Sydney and Muriel subsequently divorced, and he married May, who was pregnant with his child. Their son, Peter Sydney Ernest Lawton was born in 1923. The family initially returned to England when it was time to leave India, but the scandal of Sydney and May's affair followed them home. They were forced to move, initially to France, before finally settling in America. Their son, Peter Lawton, became a well known Hollywood actor, famously one of the Rat Pack, which included Frank Sinatra, Dean Martin, Joey Bishop and Sammy Davis Junior. He married Patricia Kennedy, sister of the future President of the United States of America, John F. Kennedy.

The war diary of the 23rd Battalion, Duke of Cambridge's Own (Middlesex) Regiment, more widely referred to as the Middlesex Regiment, shows that they were in Molini in Italy, as part of 123 Infantry Brigade, part of the 41st Division. At 1.30pm on 2 March 1918, half of the battalion left camp at Molini in Italy as part of a convoy of motorised trucks, on their way to Campo di Marte railway station in Florence, to catch a train to Bolognia. The officer in charge was Major Poole DSO, and the group included 13 officers and 489 men, six of whom were officially recorded as being sick. The train eventually left Campo di Marte at 4pm.

The second half of the battalion was due to leave camp at 6.15am the following morning, but due to a delay in the trucks arriving in camp as some had broken down en route, they eventually left two hours later than they had intended, and because of this the train was then some four hours late leaving the Campo di Marte railway station. This group comprised 17 officers along with 466 men. At 6pm late that evening, the train stopped so that the men could be fed.

After a prolonged journey across Italy, the train carrying the 23rd Battalion arrived at Mondicourt, which was a picturesque village situated in the Hauts-de-France region of northern France, at 8.30am on 8 March

1918. From there the men marched the short distance to their billets at the village of Guillemont, which some eighteen months earlier had been fought over by British and German forces during the Somme campaign, in a battle which had lasted for three days between 3 and 6 September 1916 resulting in an Allied victory.

The rest of the day was spent at a sedate pace, with the men relaxing whilst cleaning and checking their equipment. The following day was somewhat different. After breakfast there were company parades, inspection and drill, followed by another parade just before lunch at 11.45am which saw all of the regiment's different sections inspected in fighting order by the commanding officer. In the afternoon, after a short break for lunch, they had an hour's physical training.

Sunday, 10 March 1918 was allocated as a day of rest, where other than having to attend a 'voluntary' church service at nearby Humbercourt, the rest of the day was the men's to do with as they liked. For most, this meant some much needed sleep, letter writing to their loved ones back home and catching up on the latest news and gossip. Little did they know just how precious that day of rest was going to be, as the following week was full on, with tactics, exercises and rifle practice on the ranges at the village of Lucheux.

The week had also seen twenty-five men from the other ranks 'evacuated' due to unspecified sickness, but only sixteen reinforcements had joined the ranks of the Middlesex Regiment as replacements.

The following week commencing Monday, 18 March 1918, saw subtle changes, which the men would have quickly picked up, realising that they were getting very close to being in the thick of the fighting. As an officer, Walter Tull would have been slightly more in the know about what was going on than his men, but he would not have wanted them alarmed unnecessarily. By now he was 29 years of age, a few years older than most of the men under his command. They would have been looking to him for strength, direction and inspiration for what they knew would soon be expected of them. Some of these young men would not have previously been anywhere near the fighting, let alone having fired a shot in anger or seen a dead body. Part of the reason for keeping them busy with drill, exercises, training and inspections, was to take their minds off things and to stop them worrying about the task ahead.

Little did any of them know that 21 March was the start of the massive German assault known as the *Kaiserschlacht* or Emperor's battle. With divisions transferred from the Eastern Front following the Russian Revolution, this was Germany's last great attempt to win the war before the new American forces were fully engaged.

At 5.30am on that day, men of the 23rd Battalion, Middlesex Regiment, left their billets at Guillemont and marched to Mondicourt, arriving there at 7am, before catching a train to Albert, where they arrived at 3.45pm. The officers and men then had to endure yet another march to their newly allocated billets at Bouzincourt, having been on the road for more than twelve hours. The effort had seen four of their number evacuated due to sickness.

The following morning saw Walter and his men on the move again, this time they had to march to Achiet-le-Petit, via Miramont. Whilst en route at 2pm they stopped at the side of the road and ate their lunch, before continuing on their way. By now the time was 3.30pm and the next stage of their journey was by lorries, which allowed the men some rest. Their next destination was on the Arras to Bapaume Road where they bivouacked in a field until midnight when they formed up and marched to Beugny via Fremicourt where they took up support positions. On their arrival the battalion was quickly dispersed to shelters and hastily dug trenches, with the last of the men getting to sleep at dawn. The battalion headquarters was set up in a cellar at Beugny.

The war diary for the 23rd Battalion shows a number of casualties. Sadly, during the First World War, casualties from the other ranks were very rarely named, even if they were killed, but officers were, even if they were only wounded. A German artillery shell landed in their midst which resulted in eight men being killed outright, a further twelve who were wounded, with two more recorded as being missing. One officer, Second

Lieutenant S.R. Hylands was wounded. Eight other men who had previously been evacuated due to sickness, re-joined the battalion, which in part helped to counter balance some of the casualties incurred that day.

At 10.30am on Saturday 23 March the centre of the village of Beugny and the men of the 23rd Battalion experienced a sustained and heavy German artillery bombardment, after which they attacked the battalion's defensive positions to the left of the village. The attack was so effective that the men of the Middlesex Regiment were forced to retire so that they remained in line with their friends and colleagues on both their right and left flanks. Men from D Company covered the 'retirement', (it was noticeable that the word retirement was used rather than the more obvious word of retreat) with a combination of rapid rifle fire and some effective use of their Lewis guns. The result was that the German attack was repelled and a new defensive line was taken up at Beugny–Fremicourt Road. The men were eventually relieved on the night of 23/24 March and bivouacked near the aerodrome at Favreiul.

The battalion's casualties for 23 March were recorded as being three men from the other ranks killed, another twelve who were missing, thirty-six wounded, one man missing believed killed, and three who were believed to be missing and wounded.

With all of the commotion, noise and uncertainty which existed after such contacts, it was not always possible for the officers to be totally correct in their recording of casualties, especially when it came to those who were shown as missing. This could just as easily mean that they had been taken prisoner by the Germans, were lying wounded in no man's land, had sunk in the mud and water filled shell holes, or had simply been blown to pieces by a German shell.

At 11.30am on Sunday 24 March, men of the 23rd Battalion formed the reserve line near Favreuil. Late in the afternoon the front line commenced a 'retirement', and on reaching the reserve line, they were re-organised and placed into position in the battalion's sector. About 9pm that evening orders were received to withdraw and to form a new defensive line. The work to achieve this continued throughout the day, into the night, and wasn't fully completed until dawn on 25 March; it took every man who could be spared, plus some from the Royal Engineers. Casualties for 24 March were recorded as 13 men from the other ranks killed, 57 wounded, 6 missing, with a further 6 who were missing believed to have been killed, and 22 who were missing believed to have been wounded.

The entry in the war diary of the 23rd Battalion, Middlesex Regiment for Monday 25 March, began with an entry timed at 8am. Sadly, Walter and some of the men under his command, would not be alive by the end of the day. Here is the entry in its entirety:

'*8am – Shelling of our lines commenced. Enemy attacked shortly afterwards compelling the troops to withdraw across the ARRAS-BAPAUME ROAD to the line held by the Battalion. The enemy continued to push forward in massed formation. It was not until the units on both left and right had retired that the Battalion commenced an orderly withdrawal by platoons. Casualties were heavy and the enemy reached the trenches in considerable numbers as Battalios HQ commenced to withdraw. During the day other lines were taken up (1) Along the railway embankment behind BIHUCOURT. (2) At AICHET-LE-PETIT. The division was relieved during the night 25/26th. The Battalion assaulted via BUCQUOY at GOMMECOURT and took up a reserve line in old trenches there for the night.*

Casualties on the 25th. 13 killed, 61 wounded, 30 missing, 1 missing believed killed, 7 missing believed wounded.

Killed: 2nd Lt W D Tull, 2nd Lt T J Pitty

Wounded: A/Captain W Hammond, MC. Lieut. R A Green. 2nd Lt. G Barton.

Missing believed killed: Lt-Col. A R Haig-Brown, DSO.

Missing: A/Captain B T Foss, MC.

Evacuated Sick: 2nd Lt. J Jennings.'

The bodies of those men who were recovered, were buried close to where they had fallen. Sadly, Walter Tull's body was never found. It's clear to see from the war diaries of the 23rd Battalion, Middlesex Regiment, that the last three or four days of Walter's life were extremely busy ones, whether it was training, moving from location to location across the Western Front, or engaged in fighting the Germans.

The remaining six days of March 1918 passed without any real change in the battalion's fortunes. On 26 March they moved to Bienvillers, where they were bivouacked for the night and provided with their first hot meal in days. By the end of that day one soldier was missing, and Lieutenant E.L. Grear had to be sent back to England because of sickness. The following day the battalion was on the move again, this time to Gommecourt, but no sooner had they arrived there than they were on the move again. Under the cover of darkness, they moved in to trenches at Essarts. Then on 28 March they moved forward and took up positions in the support trenches at Ablainzeville, where they remained for three days before moving in to the front line trenches at the same location. By the end of that day five men had been wounded, whilst another was reported as missing believed wounded.

In a thirteen day period between 19 and 31 March 1918, the Middlesex Regiment lost a total of 396 officers and men, who were either killed in action or who subsequently died of their wounds. The worst day for casualties was 25 March 1918, the day that Walter Tull was killed in action, when a total of 91 officers and men of the Middlesex Regiment were either killed or died. One of these men, Lance Corporal (265544) Godfrey Thomas James, who was 23 years of age and served with D Company, 1st/9th Battalion, was killed in action during fighting in what was then called Mesopotamia, the latter day Iraq, and is buried in the Baghdad (North Gate) War Cemetery. The remaining ninety men all lost their lives on the Western Front, of these fifty-three have no known grave, with thirty-one commemorated on the Arras Memorial, a truly impressive structure, which can be found in the Pas de Calais region of France. The names of the remaining twenty-two are recorded on the Poizières Memorial, which is situated in the Somme region of France.

19 March 1918 – 3 deaths
20 March 1918 – 3 deaths
21 March 1918 – 15 deaths
22 March 1918 – 26 deaths
23 March 1918 – 40 deaths
24 March 1918 – 75 deaths
25 March 1918 – 91 deaths
26 March 1918 – 60 deaths
27 March 1918 – 28 deaths
28 March 1918 – 36 deaths
29 March 1918 – 7 deaths
30 March 1918 – 7 deaths
31 March 1918 – 5 deaths

Here are the ninety other officers and men who were either killed in action or died of their wounds on 25 March 1918, the same day that Walter Tull was killed. I have listed them in order of rank and then alphabetically.

Lieutenant Colonel Alan Roderick **Haig-Brown**
Captain Roy **Launceston**, 34 years of age
Captain Hugh Neville **Wegg**, 36 years of age
Lieutenant William Hugh David **De Pass**, 25 years of age
Lieutenant Rupert Anthony **Green**, 34 years of age
Lieutenant Karl Edwin **Stuart**, 27 years of age
Second Lieutenant George William **Ball**. 20 years of age
Second Lieutenant Alexander Frederick **Liversedge**
Second Lieutenant Thomas John **Pitty**, 23 years of age
Second Lieutenant Julius Brinkley **Shaw**
Second Lieutenant Albert Edward **Tillett**, 24 years of age

Serjeant G/15628 John W. **Cable**, 28 years of age.

Serjeant G/4635 Frank **Dickinson**

Serjeant L/14849 W. **Lovell**

Serjeant TF/235373 Henry John Charles **Sawtell**, 22 years of age.

Corporal L/12953 Alfred Joseph **Biele**

Lance Corporal G/10648 Ernest **Blamires**

Lance Corporal 12360 E. **Burford**

Lance Corporal G/28215 John C. **Clarke**

Lance Corporal G/52931 Charles **De Cort**, 19 years of age

Lance Corporal 265544 Godfrey Thomas **James**, 23 years of age

Lance Corporal TF/241241 Lenox J. **Sirett**

Lance Corporal 18573 G.C. **Trott**

Lance Corporal G/34384 Alfred John **Webster**, 24 years of age

Lance Corporal G/60112 Thomas **Wilde**.

Private G/52892 George Harry **Allen**, 20 years of age

Private G/F/2197 James **Allen**

Private F/3112 Henry James **Andrews**, 23 years of age

Private G/53133 Joseph Douglas **Aylett**, 19 years of age.

Private G/19766 George W. **Baston**

Private G/52901 George Edmund **Bishop**

Private G/18574 Walter J. **Brassett**

Private G/60344 William **Button**

Private G/40860 John Frederick **Cheeseman**

Private G/60290 Arthur James **Chell**, 37 years of age

Private G/33826 Eric B. **Clark**

Private G/52918 Ernest **Curl**, 19 years of age.

Private 53158 R.G. **Dackombe**, 18 years of age

Private G/44233 Cyril **Danby**, 24 years of age

Private TF/200708 Percy R. **Darlow**

Private 242139 J.T. **Day**

Private G/25577 Harry **Dean**

Private L/16525 T.S.C. **Dent**, 20 years of age

Private G/12683 Jack **Diamondstone**, 26 years of age

Private 52036 W. **Dickman**

Private Harold G. **Diggon**, 37 years of age

Private G/71820 Richard J. **Downey**

Private G/40509 Lionel Maurice **Fryer**, 29 years of age

Private G/40983 Ernest W. **Fulcher**

Private G/13764 Alfred **Gater**, 39 years of age

Private 52951 A.S. **Gates**

Private TF/235300 Fred **Genders**

Private 52480 Norman **Haggas**

Private G/21887 George Henry **Harding**, 22 years of age

Private G/20186 Bertie J. **Harris**

Private G/43171 George William **Harrison**

Private 33816 Herbert John **Howe**, 36 years of age

Private G/11494 Henry John **King**, 32 years of age

Private G/12984 Louis Irwin **Kirk**, 31 years of age

Private TF/207943 John **Keevil**

Private G/52031 J. **Kershaw**, 35 years of age

Private G/89173 George Matthew **Knowles**, 19 years of age

Private G/8802 George Henry **Lawrence**, 19 years of age

Private G/50819 J.G. **Lillicrap**

Private G/86395 William R. **Lowe**, 19 years of age

Private G/41441 Victor **Masters**

Private TF/202278 Charles **McLaughlin**, 35 years of age

Private 3136 Lionel Joseph John **Penfold**. 24 years of age

Private G/42318 Frank **Pocock**, 35 years of age

Private G/52270 Harold **Poppleton**

Private 26723 R. **Plunkett**, 24 years of age

Private G/42731 Percy E. **Relf**

Private G/14395 Percy **Ridgewell**

Private G/87420 Robert **Rowe**

Private TF/241241 William **Simmins**

Private G/53053 William H. **Smith**, 19 years of age
Private G/40187 Frederick **Stocker**
Private G/33337 Charles D. **Stratton**
Private TF/206156 William J. **Stringer**
Private G/25234 Alfred F. **Thomas**
Private G/411 Joseph **Thompson**
Private G/40927 William J. **Timms**, 22 years of age
Private TF/205325 James **Turner**, 32 years of age
Private G/52297 Horner M. **Walker**
Private G/86405 A. **Williams**, 24 years of age
Private G/33800 Charles **Whitbread**
Private G/40458 Harry John Gustave **Wyborn**, 41 years of age.

The Regiment lost men from its 1st, 1st/9th, 2nd, 4th, 6th as well as those from the 23rd Battalion, in which Walter Tull was serving at the time of his death.

Walter's brother Edward, who had initially been with him at the children's home in Bonner Street, before being adopted and moving up to Glasgow, received a telegram from Buckingham Palace informing him of Walter's death. It read as follows:

'7h 40 OHMS BUCKINGHAM PALACE

TULL 419 ST VINCENT ST, GLW

THE KING AND QUEEN DEEPLY REGRET THE LOSS YOU AND THE ARMY HAVE SUSTAINED BY THE LOSS OF 2nd LT W D TULL IN THE SERVICE OF HIS COUNTRY. THEIR MAJESTIES TRULY SYMPATHISE WITH YOU IN YOUR SORROW = KEEPER OF THE PRIVY PURSE.'

There were further deaths in the Tull family not long after Walter's. Walter's elder brother, William Stephen Palmer Tull, died of tuberculosis on 12 March 1920 and is buried at the Cheriton Road Cemetery in Folkestone. At the time of his death he was 37 years of age and a Sapper (545340) in the Royal Engineers, a married man, having wed Gertrude Mary Boxer in November 1903. According to the 1911 Census they were living with Gertrude's mother, Mildred Boxer at 45 Princess Street, Folkestone.

On the British Army Medal Rolls Index Cards that cover the period 1914 to 1920, there are eighteen men with the name William Tull, but not one of them is shown as having served with the Royal Engineers.

William and Gertrude had four children, Doris, Mildred, Gladys and Frederick. Like his father, William also earned his living working as a carpenter. By the time the Commonwealth War Graves Commission began keeping their records after the war, William's widow Gertrude had moved and was living at 59 Greenfield Road, Folkestone.

Frederick Charles Tull died on 19 December 1926 when he was only 16 years of age. He is buried in the same cemetery near to where his father William is buried. Also buried in the same cemetery are William's parents, Daniel and Alice, and his sister Bertha, who only lived for five weeks.

A petition was submitted during the period of the Conservative/Liberal Democrat Coalition Government between 2010 and 2015. It called upon David Cameron's government to posthumously award Walter Tull the Military Cross for which he had been recommended during his time as a serving British soldier during the First World War. The recommendation for the award came from Major General Sir Sydney Lawford, who had been Walter's commanding officer during the time when he had reached the rank of Second Lieutenant. It was an award which he never received. In becoming an officer, he had also become somewhat of a conundrum. Technically, he should never have been promoted to the rank of an officer in the British Army, as the Manual of Military Law did not allow for men who were not of 'pure European descent' to become officers, and only officers at the time were entitled to be awarded the Military Cross.

Whether this was the reason or whether it was because of the colour of his skin, is not known and most probably never will be.

Sadly, the above mentioned petition, which closed on 6 November 2013, only received the support of 3,031 signatures, and once again Walter was not awarded the Military Cross.

An entry on Wikipedia about Walter Tull on this very issue and part of which is credited to Phil Vasili's book, *Walter Tull 1888-1918 – Officer, Footballer* says the following: '*and in a letter of condolence to his family, 2nd Lieutenant Pickhard said that "he had been recommended for the Military Cross and certainly earned it."*'

The entry continued: '*However, the Ministry of Defence claim that there is no record of any such recommendation in his service files in the National Archives.*'

Chapter Four

Walter Tull – Newspaper reports

Two of the main reasons why there was so much interest in Walter Tull, besides the fact that he appears to have been a very well liked individual, is because he became the first black man to lead white soldiers into battle, and also because before the war he was a well known football player.

There isn't a great deal of information available about Walter in the newspapers from his days as a soldier and an officer in the British Army. What is available is mainly reports of the football matches he played, and even those are more about the match than they are specifically about Walter. I assume because at the time, in the years preceding the First World War, the military aspect of Walter's story and its historical significance, for him and black people in general, hadn't taken place. Its true worth wasn't fully appreciated until many years after his death.

Walter's story, and what gives it real significance, is the combination of the three main aspects of his life, which set him apart from most other men; the fact that he was black, a professional footballer and a soldier and officer in the British Army, who went on to lead white British soldiers into battle during the First World War. If Walter had been white, then his story would not have been anywhere nearly as significant as it actually is. He had fought against adversity as a footballer, when having to deal with hostile away supporters, as well as some of the opposing team's players. A black man trying to join a regiment of the British Army at the outbreak of the war was often met with suspicion and was a situation which the authorities did not totally support.

Was he good enough to have played international football for England? By all accounts he most definitely was, but what the football authorities thought of such a prospect is unknown. It was November 1978 before a black man was selected to represent England, in the shape of Viv Anderson, against what was then Czechoslovakia, but which is now the Czech Republic and Slovakia. England won the match 1-0. At the time Anderson was playing for Nottingham Forest Football Club at right back. He went on to represent his country on thirty occasions, including the 1982 and the 1986 World Cup tournaments.

The *Daily News* edition dated Monday, 6 September 1909, contained the following match report of the game between Everton versus Tottenham at Goodison Park, which had taken place two days earlier on 4 September. Everton deservedly won the match by a score line of four goals to two, with the Tottenham defence in particular mentioned for not covering itself in any glory, in a performance that was described as not one that would *'carry the club to success in the First Division. The forwards played quite cleverly, and compared favourably with those of Everton, and the latter were more successful mainly because of the defenders opposed to them.'*

The Tottenham goalkeeper also came in for some stiff criticism, with the article calling Boreham *'unreliable'*. On more than one occasion he failed to field the ball with his hands, and his clearances from both hands and feet left much to be desired. Three of the goals he could do nothing about, they were simply well taken shots by in form Everton players, but Freeman's goal he gifted to him.

The article was really quite brutal in apportioning blame as to who in the Tottenham side was culpable for the defeat by their poor displays. It spoke of Boreham maybe being anxious because of some of the defenders who were playing immediately in front of him, with Coquet the right back, being described as being *'woefully weak'* because of his miss-kicks and numerous missed tackles. On the other side of the field Wilkes didn't fair much better and certainly wasn't immune from the criticism. In the half backs, or what today would be referred to as the midfield, only Steel came out of the debacle with any credit and compliments. Morris was referred to as being '*too slow and easily beaten*', whilst their compatriot, Darnell, didn't do his job properly, instead going on walk about, and in doing so, leaving Wilkes badly exposed to try and deal with the two Everton players, Sharp and White, which he struggled to do on his own. This proved very costly, with two of the Everton goals coming from centres from Sharp.

The only players who came out of the game with any real credit on Tottenham's side were their forwards, Minter, Curtis, Middlemiss and Walter Tull. Minter was the main Spurs threat and although Walter didn't have an outstanding game, by any stretch of the imagination, he had a hand in both of the Tottenham goals.

The Everton defence was very strong, with Scott, Balmer and Macconachie, making few mistakes and were more than a match for the Tottenham forwards. Harris, Taylor and Makepeace in the Everton midfield proved to be stronger than their opposing counterparts, but it was Everton's Young who in particular was the pick of the bunch and the person who was effectively directing play. His ability to effortlessly glide past the opposition's players was highlighted with how easily he exposed Morris and Coquet in the Spurs defence. He repeatedly bore down on Tottenham's goal at every opportunity and was unlucky not to score.

The reporter who wrote the article spoke his mind and certainly did not hold back in his opinions, even if they didn't always appear to add up. A good example of this was his opinion of Everton's forward Freeman, whom he described as being '*the weakest forward of the lot*' even though he scored two goals, but he justified his description of the player by adding, 'the centre forward, however, succeeded in obtaining two goals, but his task on each occasion was not difficult.' The unnamed reporter was no doubt a hard man to please. If Lionel Messi had a quiet match for Barcelona but still managed to score two goals, he would more than likely be a contender for man of the match, not berated as the weakest forward on the pitch.

Tottenham were the first team to score when Walter Tull made an opening for Curtis who centred for Middlemiss to find the net with a fine shot, leaving the Everton goalkeeper, Scott, well beaten. The lead was a short lived one, with Everton scoring straight from the restart. Young and Mountford easily outwitted Morris and Coquet, before Mountford crossed for White to fire home from close range. A few minutes later Everton scored again, this time after Young beat Morris, Coquet and Steel in quick succession and, despite the close attention of Wilkes, he drew Boreham off his line and placed the ball wide of the keeper and into the back of the Spurs net, making the half-time score 2-1 to Everton.

Tottenham drew level early in the second half with a cleverly taken goal by Minter after a Spurs counter-attack which involved Walter Tull, but the inevitable outcome was always a case of when rather than if, and with Everton having the better of the first half, and total control of the entire second half, they ran out deserved winners by four goals to two, a score line which could have easily resulted in a much heavier defeat for Tottenham if Everton had converted only half of the other chances which came their way.

Unlike some previous newspaper reports of Tottenham matches in which Walter was playing, this one contained absolutely no reference to the colour of skin.

Private (F/2348) Thomas Billingham of the Middlesex Regiment was in Northampton on Saturday, 12 January 1918, visiting his family whilst home on leave from Italy. In the years before the war he had played in goal for Northampton Town's reserves, but in August 1914, he was actually playing for Leicester Fosse. Thomas and Walter knew each other well from their pre-war footballing days, and it must have been strange for them both when Thomas had to address him as 'Sir' rather than by his name.

Thomas was a physical training instructor, helping to keep his comrades as fit as was possible in the circumstances. He commented about how cold it was where they were stationed, but that warmer weather was due by the end of February, which pleased him greatly, as he would have returned to Italy after his leave by then. Thomas told a newspaper reporter that Walter Tull was also in Italy with him and that he had been promoted to the rank of second lieutenant. The pair had been part of a section, led by Walter, that had taken part in a raid on German positions on 26 December 1917 when they managed to capture three German prisoners.

It was noticeable that when the reports of Walter's death started appearing in the newspapers, he was not afforded any special treatment or any additional coverage than other officers or men from the other ranks, who had also been killed.

Private Thomas Billingham was one of those with Walter Tull when he was killed and, along with a few of his colleagues, attempted to try and recover his body. Unfortunately, they were unable to do so because of the ferocity and accuracy of the German machine gunners; to have continued with their brave efforts would have simply led to their own demise.

An interesting article appeared in the *Northampton Mercury* newspaper dated Friday 27 October 1927, some nine years after Walter Tull's death. It was about Joe Webster who was a trainer at Northampton Town Football Club and who had passed away in Northampton General Hospital on Saturday, 15 October 1927. By all accounts he was a man who was liked and well thought of by all who knew him. He had also been a professional footballer and during the 1913-1914 season, whilst playing for Watford, he was selected to play in goal for the Southern League against the Irish League in a match played in Dublin, as well as a match against the Scottish League in Glasgow. In the same season he also kept goal in the International trial match, for the South against the North.

During the First World War he had served in the army and had been wounded. Whilst serving in the Footballers' Battalion, he had met George Frederick Lessons, who was known by his middle name of Frederick, an old Northampton Town centre forward, who immediately before the war was playing with Nottingham Forest. The two had met only a week before the ex-Cobblers centre forward was killed. Three other Northampton Town players who he discovered were in the same unit as he was, were Walter Tull, Tim Coleman and George Whitworth.

Although the article mentions that Lessens had been killed in the war, there was no mention of Walter's death.

George Frederick Lessens was 34 years of age and a Lance Corporal (23563) in the 1st Battalion, Northamptonshire Regiment when he was killed in action on 7 September 1918, during the final push to victory. He is buried at the British Cemetery in the French village of Éterpigny, in the Pas de Calais region of France. At the time of his death, George's home was at 160 Noel Street, Nottingham, where his wife, Ethel, and their young son Frederick lived. When he was playing for Northampton Town, along with his friend and team mate Walter Tull, he was living at 65 Derby Road, Northampton. In his will he left £247. If George had survived the war, the chances are, because of his age, he wouldn't have played professional football many more years, if at all, on his return.

Chapter Five

Northampton Town players
who served during the war

I have already spoken about Walter Tull and Fred Lessens having served during the First World War, but there were other Northampton Town players who also served their country. Some of them made it back home, whilst others paid the ultimate price.

Harold Arthur Redhead was a local man, born in Northampton. With the outbreak of the war he enlisted in the Army. He was 27 years of age and a lieutenant attached to the 6th Battalion, Northamptonshire Regiment when he was killed in action on 7 August 1918. He is buried in the Dive Copse British Cemetery in Sailly-le-Sec, in the Somme region of France. He had also served with the 8th (Service) Battalion and the 3rd (Reserve) Battalion of the Northampton Regiment as well as the Coldstream Guards.

As a younger man he had studied to become an architect. His parents, Arthur and Annie Redhead, lived at 160 Abington Avenue, Northampton. Harold's younger brother, Cyril Howard Redhead, also saw service during the war, enlisting on 30 August 1916, his eighteenth birthday, at Northampton, with the Royal Fusiliers. He was a private (TR/10/61183) in the 28th (Reserve) Battalion. Before the war he had worked as a bank clerk. On 5 May 1917 he was posted to the 5th Battalion, Officer Cadet Corps, and just over three months later on 28 August 1917, he was discharged on being granted a commission as a second lieutenant in the 3rd (Service) Battalion, Manchester Regiment.

After the war Cyril went on his travels, as Outward Bound Passenger Lists record that he went to both Canada and South Africa, before finally returning to England on 23 July 1938. He died in 1979, aged 81.

Frank Taylor, a private with the 17th (Service) Battalion, Middlesex Regiment, which was the same one as Walter Tull, had also played for Northampton Town. He survived the war.

A number of ex-Northampton Town players also served during the war.

George Huntley Badenoch had played for Heart of Midlothian in the Scottish League, Glossop, Watford, Tottenham Hotspur, Northampton Town. Like Walter Tull, he had transferred from being a Spurs player to a Cobbler in Northampton. After leaving the latter he emigrated to Canada with his family. He was a private (19169) in the 9th Battalion, Canadian Infantry when he was killed in action on 15 June 1915 during the fighting north of the La Bassée Canal. He has no known grave and his name is commemorated on the Vimy War Memorial which is situated in the Pas de Calais region of France. His parents, Alexander and Jean Badenoch, and his wife Ellen Badenoch, all lived in Saskatchewan, Canada.

Robert Pollock Bonthron who was known to his friends as Bob, was born in Burntisland, Scotland in 1884. His footballing career began with Airdrieonians in the Scottish League. From there he moved on to Birmingham where he was in March 1911, as he appears in the census of that year lodging with Thomas and Jane Pinton at 114 Blake Lane, Bordesley Green, Birmingham.

The rest of his professional sporting life would see him yo-yo backwards and forwards between his native country and England. He left Birmingham for Dundee, then it was on to Manchester United, the team he left to join Northampton Town. Raith Rovers were next on the list of teams that he joined, before ending his playing career at his seventh and final club, Sunderland.

He had married his sweetheart, Grace Reed, in Glasgow on 16 July 1909, with their daughter, also Grace, being born the following year. The outbreak of the First World War saw him enlist in the Army at 33 years of age, initially as a private (S/7426) with the 1st, 2nd and 3rd (Reserve) Battalions, Gordon Highlanders, on 16 November 1914 in Kirkcaldy, Fife, before transferring to the 259th Area Employment Company, Labour Corps on 11 September 1917, where he was promoted to lance corporal (386526).

The website www.footballandthefirstworldwar.org shows that he was killed during the war, but there is no record of him on the Commonwealth War Graves Commission website, however his British Army Service Record survived. He first arrived in France on 14 March 1915 having left from Southampton the previous day. He had been there for less than four months when he was struck down with influenza. On 2 July 1915 he was initially treated by the 23rd Field Ambulance Unit, before being transferred the next day to the 1st Canadian Casualty Clearing Station. Still his symptoms worsened and he was transferred to the 3rd Stationary Hospital at Rouen, believed to be suffering with nephritis. The hospital staff then suspected that it might be enteric fever. Late the same day, 10 July 1915, it was confirmed he was in fact suffering with a severe case of enteric fever. His treatment continued, but still there was no improvement in his condition, so on 5 August 1915 he was moved to the 9th General Hospital in Rouen.

On 21 August he was sent back to England on board HM Hospital Ship *St Andrews*. It was nearly seven months before he was once again fit enough to return to full duties with his unit, arriving Le Havre on 6 March 1916, but after having been there for only five days, he was once again struck down by influenza, and on 11 March he was admitted to the 2nd General Hospital. His condition quickly improved and he was up and around by the end of the month.

He survived the war and was finally demobilised from the Army on 22 February 1919, at which time his home address was shown as being at 51 Parliamentary Road, Glasgow, Scotland.

On the website www.findagrave.com it shows a date of death for Robert of 14 May 1914 who is buried in Burntisland cemetery. The chances of this not being the same person as the one I have been writing about, are remote, especially if one accepts that Robert's Army Service Record is correct. The fact that he is not shown on the Commonwealth War Graves Commission website as a wartime casualty, would suggest that his subsequent death must have taken place after 1921 when war related deaths were no longer attributable to being a war time casualty.

Harry Hanger was born in Kettering in 1886. In the years before the war he was a professional footballer who played for Bradford City, Crystal Palace, and finally, Northampton Town. The 1911 Census shows him lodging with the Avery family at 12 Woodland Hill, Upper Norwood, South East London, which is no doubt when he was playing for Crystal Palace, which means that he was at Northampton Town during the same time that Walter Tull was at the club.

He enlisted early in the war and became a private (L/90) in the 5th (Royal Irish) Lancers and first arrived in France on 6 October 1914. He was killed in action on the Western Front on 23 March 1918, two days before the death of Walter Tull. He has no known grave and his name is commemorated on the Pozières Memorial.

Harold Thomas Springthorpe was born in Tinwell, Lincolnshire. In the years before the First World War, he earned his living as a professional football player, turning out for both Grimsby Town and Northampton Town. After the outbreak of war he enlisted and was a lance corporal (1803) in the 1st/1st Battalion, Lincolnshire Yeomanry. He was killed on 3 November 1915, on board the SS *Mercian*, which was attacked by the German submarine *U-38*.

The *Mercian*, had been requisitioned at the outbreak of the war and turned from a cargo ship into a troopship which carried both horses and men. This particular journey saw her en route from the United Kingdom to Oran, in North Africa. After having stopped off at Gibraltar, she left there on 3 November 1915 and continued her journey.

It was a warm sunny day in the calm waters of the Mediterranean Sea as the *Mercian* slowly made her way to her destination. In the early afternoon a shell was heard overhead, and the carefree and relaxed atmosphere on board suddenly disappeared. This was quickly followed by a second, both missing the *Mercian*, but no one on board knew where the shells were coming from to begin with. At last they spotting the *U-38* sailing on the surface on their port side. A third shell found its goal, more hits followed as the ship's captain did his best to take evasive action, but to no avail and without the ability to return fire as they had no guns on board.

For some unknown reason, the *U-38* suddenly stopped firing her guns and dived beneath the waves. This allowed the *Mercian* to make good her escape and reach Oran under her own steam. By the end of the day twenty-three troopers, including Harold, and a number of horses had been killed.

Although some Lincolnshire men were buried at Oran, Harold's body was never recovered, and his name is commemorated on the Helles Memorial in Turkey.

Arthur Harrison Allard Vann, known to his friends as Harry, was born in Bugbrooke, Northamptonshire in 1885. Before the war he had been a professional footballer, playing for Burton United, Derby County and latterly, Northampton Town.

Although initially reported as missing in action, it was subsequently confirmed that he was killed in action on 25 September 1915 during the Battle of Loos in France, at which time he was a captain and adjutant in the 12th (Service) Battalion, Prince of Wales's Own (West Yorkshire) Regiment. He had previously served as a private (1799) in the 1st/28th (County of London) Battalion (Artist's Rifles). He has no known grave but his name is commemorated on Loos Memorial. Arthur had three brothers, Reginald H. Vann, Alban H. Vann and the heroic Bernard William Vann.

Bernard William Vann was a lieutenant colonel with the 8th Battalion, Sherwood Foresters (Nottinghamshire and Derby Regiment) attached to the regiment's 1st/6th Battalion. He had also been a professional footballer who, like his brother Arthur, played for Burton United, Derby County and Northampton Town. What made Bernard even more remarkable was that in 1912 he had been ordained as a priest, which meant he was exempt from having to undergo military training. On the outbreak of war, he volunteered as an army chaplain but, frustrated by difficulties and delays, he enlisted in the infantry instead, initially in the Artists' Rifles.

Bernard was awarded the Victoria Cross, as well as the Military Cross and Bar, was twice Mentioned in Despatches, and was also awarded the *Croix de Guerre* (France). Born on 9 July 1887, in Rushden, Northamptonshire, he was killed in action on 3 October 1918 at Ramicourt in France.

The citation for his Victoria Cross, which appeared in the *London Gazette* on 14 December 1918, read as follows:

> 'For most conspicuous bravery, devotion to duty and fine leadership during the attack at Bellenglise and Lehaucourt, on September 29th 1918. He led his battalion with great skill across the Canal du Nord through very thick fog and under heavy field and machine guns. On reaching the high ground above Bellenglise the whole attack was held up by fire of all descriptions from the front and right flank. Realising that everything depended on the advance going forward with the barrage, Col. Vann rushed up to the firing line and with the greatest gallantry led the line forward. By his prompt action and absolute contempt for danger the whole situation was changed, the men were encouraged and the line swept forward. Later he rushed a field gun single handed and knocked out three of the detachment. The success of the day was in no small degree due to the splendid gallantry and fine leadership displayed by this officer. Lt. Col. Vann, who had on all occasions set the highest example of valour, was killed near Ramincourt on 3rd October 1918, while leading his battalion in attack.'

Four days later he was dead, killed by the single bullet of a German sniper during fighting at Ramicourt. He is buried in the British Cemetery in the village of Bellicourt in the Aisne region of France.

Frederick Ingram Walden had the nickname 'Fanny'. Before the war he had been a professional footballer who had played for Northampton Town before being transferred to Tottenham Hotspur, like Walter Tull who had also played for both clubs, but the other way round. Frederick had started out as an Ordinary Seaman (3727) in the Royal Naval Reserve, but enlisted in the Royal Naval Air Service as an air mechanic 2nd Class (F19237) on 15 August 1916, and was posted to the No.1 Balloon School at Blandford. He transferred to the Royal Air Force Reserve on 10 February 1919 and was discharged on 30 April 1920.

Frederick Whittaker was born in Burnley in 1886. In his career as a professional footballer, he played for five different clubs. He began with his home town club, Burnley in 1905, as a winger, when he was only 19 years of age. During the three years that he was with them he played a total of sixty games and scored twenty-one goals. In the 1908 – 1909 season he was transferred to Bradford City where he played nine games and scored one goal. The following season he transferred to Northampton Town where he spent three years, and was there at the same time as Walter Tull. He then spent two years with Exeter City, during which time he played sixty-eight games and scored seventeen goals.

In 1914 Exeter City toured South America during which Frederick Whittaker played in every one of the matches, scoring a total of five goals. The tour was most notable for the game Exeter played against a Brazilian representative side, which is now accepted as being Brazil's first ever game, which the hosts won 2-0. Because of the heat, which the Exeter players would not have been used to, four of their team actually wore hats during the match.

When war was declared on 4 August 1914, Exeter City were at sea on their way back home to England. As they neared their destination and the safety of a home port, the story goes that as they approached the area of the English Channel, they twice had shots fired across their bows by French warships, unsure as to the nationality of their vessel.

All fifteen of the Exeter City players who toured South America in 1914, either served in the armed forces during the war or in munitions factories, every one of them doing their bit for the war effort. One of these was Billy Smith. Of those who survived the war he must rank as being one of the unluckiest. The day after the signing of the Armistice, Billy was in France. Somehow he was shot in the leg, how or by whom is not known, but sadly the following year, the leg had to be amputated, and that was the end of his football career.

During the 1914-1915 season, the last one before the outbreak of the First World War, Frederick transferred to Millwall Athletic Football Club, how many times he played for them is not known. He joined his friend Walter Tull in the 17th Battalion, Middlesex Regiment but, unlike Walter, was fortunate enough to survive the war.

According to the website www.spartacus-educational.com there were some 5,000 men playing professional football before the outbreak of the First World War, of these it is estimated that 2,000 enlisted in a branch of the military. Nine months into the war and already 122 professional footballers had reportedly already been killed, and many more would follow, including Walter Tull.

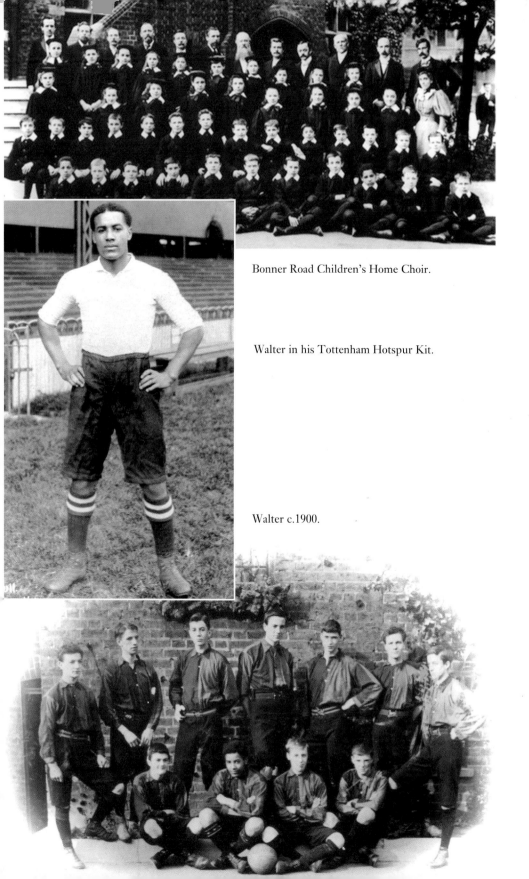

Bonner Road Children's Home Choir.

Walter in his Tottenham Hotspur Kit.

Walter c.1900.

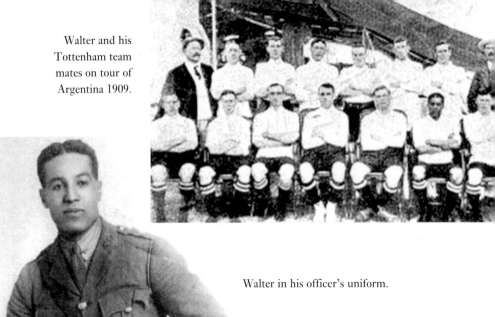

Walter and his Tottenham team mates on tour of Argentina 1909.

Walter in his officer's uniform.

Walter and fellow officers.

Walter in military uniform.

Cigarette card depicting Walter in his Northampton playing days.

Walter in a team photograph at Northampton Town (1912 - 1913 season).

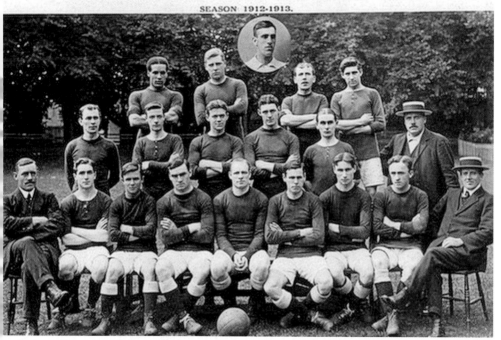

Statue of Walter Tull.

Front cover of programme for Tottenham v Manchester United, 11 September 1909, Walter's first home match.

Blue Plaque, Walter Tull, at 77 Northumberland Park, Trulock Road, London, N17.

Walter playing for Tottenham against Manchester United (1909 – 1910 season).

Walter's brother, Edward.

Walter and Edward together, possibly at Edward's home in Glasgow.

Family photograph of Walter including him and brother Edward.

Walter in civilian clothes, in relaxed pose.

Early family photo of Walter when his father was still alive.

Memorial to Walter outside of Northampton Town's Football Club.

Recruitment poster for the Football Battalion, Middlesex Regiment.

Walter Tull in uniform.

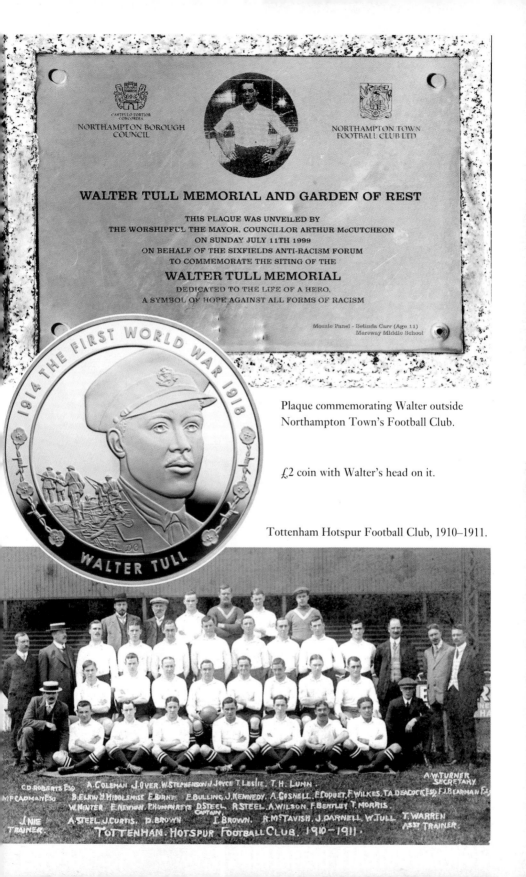

WALTER TULL MEMORIAL AND GARDEN OF REST

THIS PLAQUE WAS UNVEILED BY
THE WORSHIPFUL THE MAYOR, COUNCILLOR ARTHUR McCUTCHEON
ON SUNDAY JULY 11TH 1999
ON BEHALF OF THE SIXFIELDS ANTI-RACISM FORUM
TO COMMEMORATE THE SITING OF THE

WALTER TULL MEMORIAL
DEDICATED TO THE LIFE OF A HERO,
A SYMBOL OF HOPE AGAINST ALL FORMS OF RACISM

Mosaic Panel - Belinda Carr (Age 11)
Mereway Middle School

NORTHAMPTON BOROUGH
COUNCIL

NORTHAMPTON TOWN
FOOTBALL CLUB LTD

1914 THE FIRST WORLD WAR 1918

WALTER TULL

Plaque commemorating Walter outside
Northampton Town's Football Club.

£2 coin with Walter's head on it.

Tottenham Hotspur Football Club, 1910–1911.

Tottenham Hotspur Football Club, 1911-12.

Tottenham Hotspur Football
Club 1911–1912 season.

Middlesex Regiment Cap
badge.

Gravestone of William
Stephen Palmer Tull,
Walter's brother.

Walter in civilian clothing.

Chapter Six

Tottenham Hotspur players who served during the war

Having included a list of the names of the players from Northampton Town Football Club who had left the safety of playing football for a living, to go and serve their King and country, it seems right to list those players from Tottenham Hotspur, who also served. Those men who played for both Northampton Town and Tottenham Hotspur during the pre-war years, have already been included in the chapter on Northampton Town. All of these men would have known of Walter Tull, and some, like Billy Minter, had played in the same Tottenham team as he had during his time at the club.

Of the men who were playing for Tottenham when war broke out, and those who had previously played for them, fourteen died during the war. Besides these men I have also included a few others who survived the war and returned home.

Henry John Bagge known to his friends as Harry, was born in Tottenham who went on to join his home town club. He was a defender who had played for two other clubs, Clapton Orient, now Leyton Orient and The Wednesday, now Sheffield Wednesday, before arriving at White Hart Lane, although he never played a first team competitive match for them. 'The Wednesday' changed their name in 1929. They had began their existence as a cricket club in 1820, and 'Wednesday' became part of the club name because that was the day of the week on which they played their matches. The football side of the club was appropriately founded on a Wednesday, 4 September 1867.

Henry originally enlisted in the Royal Navy in 1915 as an Ordinary Seaman (9760), where he was posted to the Royal Naval Air Service. It was there that he discovered his love of aircraft and possibly the reason why he later transferred to the Royal Air Force, where he became an Air Mechanic 2nd Class (209760). He survived the war and was transferred to the Royal Air Force Reserve on 15 March 1919. After the war he returned to playing football with Fulham, where he made a total of 179 appearances between 1919 and 1926.

Henry became one of the first ever British managers to coach in Spain, when he went into management after his retirement from football. Between 1947 and 1949 he managed the Athletic Club, now Athletico Bilbao, which played in the Spanish first division, and between 1950 and 1952, he managed Salamanca and Linense, both playing in the Spanish second division.

George Henry Bowler was born in Derbyshire on 23 January 1890. His first football club was amateur side Gresley Rovers, the team he played for before becoming a professional footballer with Derby County Football Club in May 1911. He had two seasons at the Baseball ground, but in all that time and despite being a regular in the reserves, he only played one first team match.

The 1911 Census shows him still working as a coal miner and a hewer, living with his parents and three brothers at 29 Meadow Lane, Newhall, Derbyshire.

Despite being a reserve at Derby, George signed for Tottenham Hotspur in time for the 1913 – 1914 season, but didn't make his competitive first team debut until February 1914. It would appear that it was as a reserve that Tottenham saw him as well, because he only played in two more first team competitive matches for the club, the last of which was in April 1914 against Liverpool in a 0-0 draw at White Hart Lane.

With the outbreak of the First World War, George, like many of his colleagues, enlisted as a Private (F/27) in the newly formed 17th (1st

Football) Battalion, Middlesex Regiment, the same one that Walter Tull had joined. After completing his basic training, he arrived in France with his colleagues on 17 November 1915. George, like Walter, went on to take part in the bloody fighting of the Battle of the Somme, a battle which both of them survived.

The 17th Battalion and 23rd (2nd Football) Battalion, Middlesex Regiment, merged in February 1918, due to heavy losses, mainly incurred by the 17th Battalion. George was serving with the 23rd Battalion in France when Walter Tull was killed. Maybe he was one of the men who tried unsuccessfully to recover Walter's body from the battlefield.

On 17 June 1918 George was transferred to the 18th (County of London) Battalion, London Regiment, still as a private (45843 and 602445) where he remained until he was demobbed from the Army in early 1919.

Tottenham decided against offering George a new contract on his return from military service, and so he signed for Luton Town Football Club, but once again the best he could get was reserve team football, with first team opportunities few and far between. This eventually led to him deciding to retire from football.

John Fleming was one of the war's victims, although he did not meet his end killed by a bayonet, bomb or bullet, on the battlefields of France, he had been taken in his prime by the dreaded influenza at an Army training camp at Richmond in Yorkshire. Born in Stirlingshire, Scotland in 1890, his father was a mining contractor, but for young John, it was to be a healthier pastime that would earn him his living. He utilised his sporting prowess and turned to football, playing for five clubs in Scotland before moving across the border into England in 1911 and signing for Newcastle United at the age of 21. In the 1911 – 1912 season John only managed to make the first team on four occasions, mainly due to injuries. This was in an era when there was no such thing as substitutes.

He moved on to Tottenham in time for the beginning of the 1913 – 1914 season, but after making eight appearances in the last two months of the year, injury struck again causing him to miss the rest of the season. It would be nine months before he next appeared in Tottenham's first team, and by the end of the 1914 – 1915 season he had returned to Scotland with the mighty Glasgow Rangers. By now the First World War was in full swing and John decided that he had to do his bit. He enlisted in the Cameron Highlanders and at the time of his death on 21 March 1916, he was a Lance Corporal in the Regiment's 8th (Reserve) Battalion, still undergoing his basic training. He is buried in Inveresk Parish churchyard in Musselburgh.

John's brother William also signed for Tottenham in August 1914, which saw them both on the club's books at the same time.

John Joseph Hebdon was born at Portsmouth, Hampshire, in 1895, but by 1911 he was living with his parents and nine brothers and sisters at 10 Mansford Buildings, Mansford Street, Bethnal Green Road, Bethnal Green, London, the same area where Walter Tull had lived for most of his young life in the children's home.

By 1911, John had left school and was working as a furniture porter in Bethnal Green, but it was his footballing abilities that eventually brought him the job that he really wanted. After playing for a local amateur side he came to the attention of Tottenham Hotspur Football Club and by the outbreak of the war he had already signed professional terms with them. By the time he had attested at Edmonton on 6 December 1915, and been placed on the Army Reserve, he had yet to play a first team match for the club. He was not mobilised for military service for another four months, when he was called up on 6 April 1916 and became a private (7473) in the 14th (County of London) Battalion, London Regiment (London Scottish). His home then was at 37 Batham Road, Edmonton, Middlesex.

Having completed his basic training, he was sent out to France with his battalion, arriving there on 29 July 1916. Theirs was an almost immediate baptism of fire for John and his comrades with their involvement in the

Battle of the Somme, along with some of the other battles which took place on the Western Front throughout the latter part of 1916 and early 1917.

His Army Service Record strangely shows his occupation as that of a second salesman and not a professional footballer.

He was killed in action on 9 April 1917, by which time he had reached the rank of lance corporal (513412). The War Diaries for the 14th Battalion, London Regiment, show that they were on the outskirts of Neuville-Vitasse, preparing to attack the village as part of the early stages of the Battle of Arras.

'At 1.120 am the London Scottish left their final assembly trenches and advanced to the attack of that portion of the COJEUL SWITCH system which lay between the NEUVILLE VITASSE – WANCOURT Rd, on the right and the NEUVILLE VITASSE – FEUCHY Road on the left. This portion of the COJTEUL SWITCH consisted of three trenches, TELEGRAPH Hill trench being the front trench, CARD trench being the centre trench, and BACK trench, the rear trench.

The distance of the objective from the assembly trenches, was approximately 1400yds. The battalion attacked with 3 Coys, the remaining company being kept in reserve.'

The diary entry is extremely detailed, outlining the overall success of the operation and ends with the following sentence.

'During the operations detailed above, the casualties to the Battalion were 3 officers wounded, 17 OR killed, 66 OR wounded, 44 OR missing.'

John was one of the seventeen other ranks who were killed. He is buried at the London Cemetery in the village of Neuville-Vitasse, which is situated in the Pas de Calais region of France.

Alf Hobday had been a soldier in the British Army during the early years of the twentieth century, joining the 1st Battalion, Northumberland Fusiliers in 1904, as Private 377, his service being mainly in India. After having served for eight years, he left the Army in 1912 and was placed on the Army Reserve, meaning that when he signed for Tottenham Hotspur in May 1913, he was still in that position. Soon after the outbreak of war, Alf, not surprisingly in the circumstances, was one of the first to be called up as part of the British Expeditionary Force and arrived in France with his old battalion on 14 August 1914, having been promoted to the rank of sergeant and keeping his original service number of 377.

Alf was straight in the thick of things and saw action at Mons, Le Cateau, The Marne, The Aisne, La Bassée, Messines and the First Battle of Ypres. He was killed in action on 16 June 1915 when his battalion launched an attack on German positions as part of the Battle of Bellewaarde. His body was never recovered and his name is commemorated on the Ypres Memorial, which is situated in the West-Vlaanderen region of Belgium. On the same day that Alf Hobday lost his life, 146 colleagues of his from the 1st Battalion, Northumberland Fusiliers, were also killed. Out of all these a staggering 143 also have no known grave.

Edward John 'Teddy' Lightfoot was another who was at Tottenham during Walter Tull's time at the club. He enlisted in the Royal Garrison Artillery in 1916 at Seaforth, Lancashire, was posted to the 1st Siege Battery, and went on to become a Serjeant (168781).

He was 30 years of age when he was killed in action on 20 July 1918 and is buried at the Military Cemetery at Esquelberg, a village close to the French border with Belgium. The Commonwealth War Graves Commission website shows him as being John Edward Lightfoot, and a report in the *New York Times* newspaper, dated 19 October 1918, refers to him as being E.D. Lightfoot.

William James Minter, more commonly known as 'Billy', had been a team mate of Walter Tull's at Tottenham before Walter left and signed for Northampton Town. Billy's footballing career had seen him play for Norwich City, Reading, Woolwich Arsenal, with which he had signed in 1905, soon after leaving the Army, and then in May 1908 he signed for arch North London rivals, Tottenham. A player transferring between these two clubs is very rarely appreciated by either set of fans.

Like Alf Hobday, Billy had previously served in the British Army, initially as a Gunner (24239) with the Royal Field Artillery, before later transferring at the same rank (23572) to No.17 Company, Royal Garrison Artillery. He was discharged by purchase on 22 February 1907 at Sheerness in Kent, which in essence meant he bought himself out of the Army, the cost of which at the time was £18, a sum that was normally beyond the means of the average soldier.

Billy married Elizabeth Eliza Whybrew on 2 May 1908 at St Thomas's Church in Woolwich, and the couple lived at 91 Bruce Castle Road, Tottenham. It would appear that at the time of their wedding, Elizabeth was already five months pregnant. Billy's Army Service record shows that at the time of his enlistment on 3 May 1915 at Tottenham, the couple had three children, twins William and Elizabeth, who were born on 30 August 1908, along with Dorothy, who was born six years later on 14 July 1914. He wasn't shown as being a professional football player, but a wheelwright.

With the First World War some nine months old Billy enlisted in the Army for a second time on 3 May 1915 for the duration of the war, in the Royal Engineers, and was posted to the 222nd Field Company as a sapper (96001). As a result of his re-enlistment, he was entitled to a £9 refund under Army Order 99 of 1915, no doubt a sum of money that would have been greatly appreciated. He was promoted to the rank of corporal on 18 May 1915 and further promoted to sergeant just over three weeks later on 11 June, arriving in France on 18 November 1915. He was wounded on 3 October 1917.

He was awarded the Meritorious Service Medal for devotion to duty. The details of his award appeared in the *London Gazette* dated 17 June 1918.

The 1911 Census showed **Finlay (Findley) Weir** living at 285 Middlewood Road, Sheffield, South Yorkshire, where he lodged with Mr and Mrs Cottam, and another professional footballer, David McClean. This was during the time he was played for The Wednesday football club.

Finlay, enlisted in the British Army during the First World War, and became a serjeant (96038) in the Royal Engineers. At the time of his death on 9 July 1918, he was serving with the 3rd (Reserve) Battalion, a training depot based in Newark in Nottinghamshire.

The reason behind his death is not clear, but as he is buried in Lambhill Cemetery in Glasgow, it would seem that his death was either the result of an accident, illness or disease. He was not killed in action, nor did he die as a result of wounds he had received in battle whilst serving in France.

Frederick John Griffiths was born in Presteigne, Wales, on 13 October 1873 but before the war he was a barman in a hotel, living at 31 St Austen Street, Shirebrook, Mansfield with his wife Elizabeth and their six children.

After the outbreak of war Frederick enlisted and became a serjeant (20969) in the 15th (Service) Battalion, Nottinghamshire and Derbyshire (Sherwood Foresters) Regiment. He died of his wounds on 30 October 1917 in Belgium and is buried at the Dozinghem Military Cemetery, which is situated in the West-Vlaanderen region of the country.

Frederick had previously played for Tottenham, West Ham United, Preston North End and Millwall.

There was another Frederick Griffiths, who was killed on the same day, who was a gunner in the Royal Garrison Artillery.

Alan Roderick Haig-Brown had played professional football for Brighton and Hove Albion, Clapton Orient and Tottenham, the latter between 1901 – 1903.

Haig-Brown had been a military man since 1906 when he was commissioned as a lieutenant in the Lancing Officers' Training Corps. He was transferred to the 23rd (2nd Football) Battalion, Middlesex Regiment on 1 January 1916 and promoted to the rank of major. By September the same year he had been appointed a temporary lieutenant colonel and became the commanding officer of the battalion, which included Walter Tull. Destiny was to connect the two men in death as they were both killed in action on the same day, 25 March 1918. Haig-Brown was buried at the Achiet-le-Grand Communal Cemetery Extension.

John Jarvie was a Scotsman from Kirkintilloch in Glasgow who had previously played for Tottenham Hotspur. He enlisted in the Army early on in the war and became a private (S/11278) in B Company, 2nd Battalion, Princess Louise's (Argyll and Sutherland Highlanders). He was killed in action on 2 October 1916 on the Western Front in France, when a mine exploded near to his position. He was 27 years of age and is buried in the Cambrin Churchyard Extension, in the Pas de Calais region of France.

William Henry Lloyd was a proud Welshman, born in Wrexham in 1888. As a professional footballer he had played for Tottenham Hotspur, but he was already in the Army before the outbreak of the First World War. According to the 1911 Census, he was 23 years of age, a married man and a private (13107) in the 1st Battalion, Grenadier Guards, stationed at Hanover Square in London.

By the outbreak of the First World War, William was in the 2nd Battalion and was a corporal (13107). He and his colleagues arrived at Le Havre in France at 2.30pm on 13 August 1914, and then marched to a rest camp near Bléville. Just over three months later on 7 November 1914, William was dead, killed in action during fighting at Klein Zillebeke in Belgium.

The 2nd Battalion's War Diaries for 7 November 1914, record the following.

'Remain in trenches at Klein Zillebeke. 3rd and 22nd Brigades made counter attack to gain lost ground, but only partially successful. During previous night had refused our right, and taken up new and continuous line through wood, our left remaining in former positions. Shelled most of day. Enemy's infantry advanced but driven back. Maintained position. 19 killed, 46 wounded, 3 missing.'

William was one of those who were killed. He has no known grave, but his name is commemorated on the Ypres Memorial.

Alexander MacGregor was a teenager when he arrived at Tottenham, having come down from Scotland in June 1914, but at the outbreak of the war he enlisted in the Gordon Highlanders. There remains some confusion over the date and the circumstances of Alexander's death.

Archie Wilson was born in Ayrshire in 1891 and was another player who was at Tottenham at the same time as Walter Tull, arriving at the club in late 1909 as a teenager. He was sent out on loan to Southend United and Middlesbrough. Soon after the outbreak of the war Archie enlisted in the Army, joining the 1st/14th Battalion, London Regiment (London Scottish) as a private (5480). He was killed in action on 1 July 1916, the first day of the Battle of the Somme. Sadly, his body was never recovered, but his name is commemorated on the Thiepval Memorial.

Norman Arthur Wood enlisted in the British Army in February 1915, joining No.3 Company, 17th (1st Football) Battalion, Duke of Cambridge's Own (Middlesex Regiment) the same unit that Walter Tull joined. He was eventually promoted to the rank of sergeant (F/663), and was killed in action during the fighting at Delville Wood on 28 July 1916. He was 26 years of age. His body was not recovered, but his name is commemorated on the supremely impressive Thiepval Memorial, which is situated in the Somme region of France.

Chapter Eight

Other Black Soldiers and Regiments of the First World War

Although black soldiers in the British Army were rare during the First World War, there were an estimated 16,000 black men from the colonies who fought on the side of the British between 1914 and 1918, and soldiers from Nigeria, Ghana, Sierra Leone, Gambia, Malawi, Kenya and Uganda were mobilised and used to defend the borders of their own countries which bordered on to German held territories in the region.

At the outbreak of the war in August 1914, there were many men from the West Indies who made their way to England to enlist in the British Army. Those who were accepted were simply then allocated to the next particular regiment which required numbers to bring them up to strength. After a short period of time the War Office became concerned at the number of black soldiers in the British Army. The following is taken from the 'Moving Here' website.

'Following the outbreak of hostilities in 1914 many West Indians left the colonies to enlist in the Army in the UK, and were recruited into British Regiments. The War Office was concerned with the number of black soldiers in the Army and tried to prevent any people from the West Indies enlisting. Indeed, the War Office threatened to repatriate any who arrived. Eventually, after much discussion between the Colonial Office and the War Office, and the intervention of King George V, approval to raise a West Indian contingent was given on 19 May 1915. On 26 October 1915, the British West Indies Regiment was established.'

A total of 80,000 black African men fought in the American, British, French and German armies during the course of the First World War. Of these 10,000 died.

During the course of the war the **British West Indies Regiment** raised a total of eleven battalions, which consisted of 15,601 officers and men. Of these 1,397 lost their lives as a result of their involvement in the First World War.

Men of the 1st and 2nd battalions served in Egypt and Palestine. Men from the 3rd, 4th, 6th and 7th battalions served in France and Flanders. The 8th and 9th battalions also served in France and Flanders, but were sent to Italy in 1918, whilst the 9th and 10th battalions served in France and Italy. The 5th Battalion was a Reserve unit.

Eleven men died throughout the course of 1915. Two are buried at the La Clytte Military Cemetery, which is about four miles west of the town centre of Ypres in the West-Vlanderen region of Belgium. Both men died on 27 May 1915, and both were serving with the 3rd Battalion. The other nine men are all buried at Seaford Cemetery, in Sussex, the town where the regiment's 1st Battalion was formed and spent the remainder of the year. All of the deaths took place between October and December 1915, either as a result of illness or through training accidents.

The following year, 1916, saw 175 men of the regiments die in different locations across the world. In 1917 the casualties more than doubled, with a total of 463 men either being killed in action, dying of their wounds, illness or disease. The final eleven months of the war saw the death rate rise by a further 503. In the seven weeks between the signing of the Armistice and the end of the year, a further 57 men of the regiment died. Throughout 1919 a staggering 172 men are recorded as having died. The following year, however, shows only 12 men as having lost their lives.

The last year that deaths of soldiers who had served during the war were officially recorded as war related was 1921. Four of the regiment's men died that year with the last man being Corporal 10905 W.V. Byer, who died on 25 August 1921. He is buried at the St Barnabas Churchyard, in

St Michael, Barbados. He is the only man that served in the First World War, buried there who was a serving soldier at the time of his death.

Another man, Private 3133 R. Edwards, who also served with the British West Indies Regiment, is buried at the Up Park Camp, Kingston Military Cemetery, but sadly there is no exact date recorded for his death. All that is shown on the Commonwealth War Graves Commission website is that he died between 4 August 1914 and 31 August 1921.

There would undoubtedly have been some men who served with the regiment who came from Barbados who were the sons of men who had either been friends of Walter's father Daniel, or who knew him in passing.

Men from Bermuda also did their bit in support of the Allied war effort. There was the **Bermuda Volunteer Rifle Corps** which was attached to the 1st Battalion, Lincolnshire Regiment. Its members were in fact white. The Corps had been formed in 1894 as an all white, racially segregated reserve for the Regular Army's infantry aspect of the Bermuda Garrison.

The **Bermuda Garrison Artillery** on the other hand was made up of white officers, whilst the other ranks included both black and white men. Its main purpose was to defend the Royal Naval Dockyard in Bermuda and other nominated locations around the island.

On 31 May 1916 a group of 201 officers and men, under the command of Major Thomas Melville Dill, left Bermuda for deployment in France. A year later on 6 May 1917, they were joined by two fellow officers along with sixty men from the other ranks, and were amalgamated into what was known as the Bermuda Contingent, Royal Garrison. They were set to work delivering ammunition to units on the front. The unit served during the Battle of the Somme, but afterwards moved away from the front and set to working in dock areas along the French and Belgian coastline. In April 1917 they were attached to the Canadian Corps and served with them at the Battle of Vimy Ridge. They also saw action at the Third Battle of Ypres. Two of their number were awarded the Military Medal.

By the end of the war, ten members of the Bermuda Garrison Artillery had been killed whilst serving in France. The first of these men fell in 1916, six were killed during 1917, and the remainder died in 1918, with two of these deaths being after the signing of the Armistice.

The **King's African Rifles** had initially been formed in 1902. It was a British Colonial Regiment whose men came from the numerous areas owned by the British throughout East Africa. Nearly all of its officers were white men who had been seconded from long established British Army Regiments. Some of them were also black men who came from some of the British colonies in the region. The men who formed the other ranks were black Africans or Askaris. Before the war, the men of the King's African Rifles performed both a policing as well as a military role throughout East Africa. This was one of the reasons why the uniforms which they wore included a dark blue coloured jersey and puttees. With the outbreak of the war the uniform was replaced with khaki coloured items.

Black soldiers could also be found in some front line British regiments. It is known that some fought with the Northumberland Fusiliers and at least one served with the Hampshire Regiment. It is known that black recruits were not well thought of by some senior British Army officers, who saw them as being inferior to white soldiers and who believed that their presence would affect morale.

It was not just the British who had black soldiers serving in their midst, for example the French Army was extremely grateful to its Senegalese soldiers. India sent over one million men, who had volunteered to aid the British and Allied war effort in the different theatres of war. Of these an estimated 62,000 died, whilst a further 67,000 were injured. The first batch of 161,000 men from the Lahore and Meerut infantry divisions arrived on these shores in October 1914, they were both brave and proud young men and keen to do their bit. Eight of them were awarded the

Victoria Cross, the highest military honour that is available to a soldier of any rank, serving in the Army of the British or a Commonwealth nation, for bravery in the face of the enemy.

Indian soldiers were quickly in the thick of it, and saw action at the Battle of Neuve Chapelle, which took place over three days between 10 and 13 March 1915. They also saw action during the Battle of the Somme, the Battle of Flers-Courcelette and the Battle of Cambrai, to name but a few.

George Edward Kingsley Bemand was another black man and fellow officer from the First World War, who received his commission in May 1915, some two years before Walter Tull. Like Walter he was a Second Lieutenant, but he was in charge of an artillery unit in the Royal Field Artillery and was not an infantry officer.

George's story is also intriguing because, as a man whose heritage was not British, as the rules stood at the time, he should not have received a commission in the British Army as an officer. There are lots of similarities between Walter's and George's stories, even down to the fact that they were both killed in action.

George was born in Jamaica on 19 March 1892 and came to England with his mother and other siblings, arriving at Liverpool on 21 July 1908 on board the ill-fated Cunard passenger liner RMS *Lusitania*, which was sunk on Friday, 7 May 1917 by the German submarine *U-20* and was one of the main reasons for America's entry into the First World War. En route from Port Morant in Jamaica, the vessel they were on, the *Admiral Sampson,* first landed in Boston, America on 21 October 1907. They then left Boston travelling on to New York on board the *Orinoco*, arriving there on 9 July 1908 before continuing their journey on the *Lusitania*.

The family members who travelled to England were George's mother, Mary Ann Bemand, who is also referred to as Minnie, George, his brothers Vernon and Harold and his sister Elsie. The 1911 Census showed them all living at 26 Woodville Road, Ealing, West London, along with Mary's sister-in-law, Laura, and although Mary and Laura are shown as having no occupation, they are able to afford to rent the property and engage a nurse to help look after the children. By 1911 George was 19 years of age and a live-in pupil at Dulwich College in South London, before going on to University College, London, in 1913 where he studied engineering. In October 1914, soon after the outbreak of war, George joined his university's Officers' Training Corps, before applying for a commission in May 1915 with the 30th (County Palatine) Divisional Artillery. His application was supported by his commanding officer, Brigadier General Anthony John Abdy, despite him clearly knowing the restrictions preventing black men, especially those not born in England, from becoming officers in the British Army. Abdy had first been commissioned into the Royal Artillery in 1876.

In an article included on the blog, 'Great War London – London and Londoners in the First World War', is a copy of George's application to be commissioned as an officer, Abdy has written in his own hand the words, '*I am willing to take him.*' It was an indication that he held the man in very high esteem, and was in effect putting his own reputation on the line by openly supporting him. The article on the blog also makes mention of the fact that George had indicated on his application that he is of pure European descent, which was quite clearly not the case.

After completing his initial training at Grantham and Salisbury Plain, George first arrived in France on 16 August 1916 as part of 148 Brigade's Ammunition Column, but he later transferred to Y Company, 5th Trench Mortar Battery, which was attached to the 5th Division. He was killed by an exploding German shell on 26 December 1916 along with Lance Corporal 87427 F.A. Cook, who had previously been mentioned in despatches for his bravery under enemy fire and who was only 20 years of age. Both men were buried at the Le Touret Military Cemetery at Richebourg-L'Avoué, in the Pas de Calais region of France.

Just like Walter Tull, George had a brother who was a victim of the war. His younger brother Harold Leslie Bemand was a Gunner (107838) in X Company, Trench Mortar Brigade, when, according to the British Army's Register of Soldiers Effects, which covers the period between 1901–1921, he was killed in action on 7 June 1917, and is buried at the Bedford House Cemetery, near Ypres. An interesting fact about the cemetery was its location in the grounds of the Chateau Rosendal. Bedford House was a name allocated to it by the British Army. The picturesque grounds of the chateau included a moat and a small wooded park and was a location for Field Ambulance units, which was the main reason it became a cemetery.

Although the Bemand family included Harold, George, and their mother Mary, the Commonwealth War Graves Commission website shows the home address of Mary and her husband, George Bemand as St Michael's Villa, 1 Bow Street, Kingston, Jamaica. Records show that on 28 January 1912, Mary and her children, Harold, Vernon and Elsie, left England via Liverpool for Kingston, Jamaica, the first stop being Boston on the east coast of America.

Although there are similarities between Walter Tull and George Bemand, there were also noticeable differences as well. But what seems to connect them most strongly was the fact that they both became officers in the British Army at a time when only men who were white and with a proven British heritage were allowed to fulfil that role. They showed other black men what it was possible to achieve.

During the First World War, many men were given temporary commissions as second lieutenants and as such weren't seen as actual officers by some of those who had acquired the same rank by being professional soldiers. Maybe it is this very ambiguity which allowed Walter Tull and George Bemand to become officers, perhaps it was never a case of its being an oversight by the authorities, but an understanding that, as they were holding a temporary rank as an officer, the rules of being non-white or not of British heritage, simply didn't apply to somebody who was only holding a commission in a temporary capacity.

Private John Williams was a highly decorated soldier who joined the British Army in 1914 and was nicknamed 'the black VC' by his comrades. According to a report in the *African Telegraph* in 1919, his medals included the Military Medal, the Distinguished Conduct Medal, the French *Médaille Militaire* and *Légion d'Honneur* and the Cross of St George. In his photograph he has four wound stripes on his sleeve but it is not known in which regiment he served.

William Robinson Clarke was the first black pilot to fly for the Royal Flying Corps. He was born at Gregory Park, St Catherine, Jamaica on 4 October 1895. When the First World War broke out he left his home at 'Essequibo' Arnold Road, Kingston, Jamaica, and made his way to England, paying for his own passage. On arrival, he enlisted in the Royal Flying Corps on 26 July 1915. Initially he served as a 2nd Class Air Mechanic, making sure that the aircraft were air worthy and well maintained, but on 18 October that same year, he was posted to France and became a driver with a balloon observation company, but his real desire was to qualify as a pilot and fly the aircraft which it had previously been his job to repair and maintain. He applied to become a pilot and was successful in his application and began his training course in December 1916. Four months later, on 26 April 1917, having completed his training and qualified as a pilot, he was promoted to the rank of sergeant. His Royal Aero Club Aviator's Certificate recorded his nationality as being British.

He was sent to No.4 Squadron of the Royal Flying Corps, which at the time was in Abele in Belgium, carrying out reconnaissance over the German lines. On 28 July 1917 William was flying such a mission, when the RE8 Biplane which he was flying with observer Second Lieutenant F.P. Blencowe, was engaged by a large number of German aircraft. During the attack William was wounded, but even though he had been shot through the back he managed to fly his battered aircraft back to his aerodrome and landed safely. His observer, Lieutenant Blencowe was uninjured.

After the war William went to live in Canada for a while and on 17 December 1921 he crossed the border into America at Detroit, Michigan, where he stated that he intended to remain for a period of six weeks. The immigration card which he completed on his entry also recorded that he had previously worked in America between May and October 1920.

William married Gladys Kathleen Thomas on 22 October 1923 in Montreal, at the Anglican Christ Church Cathedral. They had two sons, Howard, who was born in 1926 and Reginald who was born the following year. He eventually returned to Jamaica where he saw out his days, passing away in 1981 aged 86.

David Louis Clemetson was born in Point Maria, Jamaica on 1 October 1893, into a very wealthy family of plantation owners. His father, David Robert Clemeston, owned the Frontier Estate sugar plantation, which he had inherited from his father, Robert Clemetson, who had been a slave. He was also the son of the plantation owner, who left it all to Robert when he died.

David began his education in Jamaica before moving to England and attending the Clifton College in Bristol, where he gained his first taste of military instruction when he joined the college's Officers' Training Corps, before going on to study law at Trinity College, Cambridge in 1912.

With the outbreak of war David joined the Army and being a keen sportsman, he enlisted in the 23rd (Service) Battalion, (1st Sportsman's) Royal Fusiliers (City of London Regiment), which accepted men up to 45 years of age. The battalion had been raised by Mrs E. Cunliffe-Owen at the Hotel Cecil in The Strand, London, in September 1914. Those like David who were accepted, were sent to a purpose built camp at Grey Towers in Hornchurch, Essex, to undergo their basic training. This was completed in June 1915 at which time the battalion was attached to 99 Brigade, in the 33rd Division, and sent out to France where they arrived in November 1915. Throughout the war the men of the Sportsman's Battalion saw plenty of action on the Western Front, at such battles as Vimy Ridge, The Somme and Delville Wood. Some very well known and famous sporting stars of the day had joined the Sportsman's Battalion, but possibly one of the more surprising recruits was a member of the 24th (Service) Battalion (2nd Sportsman's) who were based at Hare Hall, near Romford. His name was Sir Herbert Raphael, a Liberal Party politician and a millionaire lawyer.

David Clemetson quickly became an acting lance serjeant as his leadership qualities had already been recognised by his senior officers. So impressed were they that Clemetson was put forward for a commission by his commanding officer, Lieutenant Colonel H.J.H. Inglis. After successfully completing his course, he became a second lieutenant in the Pembroke Yeomanry, a Territorial unit, on 27 October 1915.

In March 1916 he went out to Egypt with his battalion, but was sent back to England suffering from shell-shock. The ship taking him back to England, HMHS *Dover Castle*, was attacked and sunk by the German submarine *U-67* on 26 May 1917, off the coast of North Africa. Six members of the ship's crew were killed, whilst 600 crew, staff and patients were rescued and survived. In a somewhat strange incident *U-67* fired one torpedo which killed the six members of crew. Everybody else on board was safely rescued, leaving only a skeleton crew who attempted to get the vessel back to port. An hour had now passed, and the U-boat which had remained in the vicinity to monitor the situation from beneath the waves, fired a second torpedo, causing the *Dover Castle* to sink within a matter of minutes, but not before the crew had made good their escape.

David Clemetson was one of the survivors, and after initially being picked up by HMHS *Karapara* and taken to Gibraltar, he was returned to the UK and sent to Craiglockhart Hospital in Edinburgh to recuperate. He was in good company as two of the most distinguished patients were Seigfried Sassoon and Wilfred Owen. It was in July 1917, while he was still recovering, that he received the news that he had been promoted to the rank of second lieutenant.

By the time he had fully recovered his unit was no more. It had been amalgamated with the Glamorgan Yeomanry to become the 24th (Pembroke and Glamorgan) Battalion, Welsh Regiment and had been sent to the Western Front in France, by March 1918.

Clemetson was killed in action on 21 September 1918 during the 'final push' at Peronne near St Quentin. He is buried at the Unicorn Cemetery, near the village of Vendhuile in the Aisne region of France.

It is strange that during the First World War military law forbade non-white men who did not have British heritage from becoming officers in the British Army, yet men like George Bemand, Walter Tull and David Clemetson were not only commissioned as officers, but were put forward for their commissions by their white commanding officers, who surely knew the restrictions on non-white men becoming British Army officers. Maybe it was to do with their social standing in society, wealth and academic abilities, which allowed their progression and promotion in the Army, treatment which would not have been afforded to a normal black man.

In Walter Tull's case, he was an intelligent individual who was well known by men and women from all walks of life no matter what their social standing was. Above all he had public appeal. With George Bemand, it was a case of another intelligent man who had attended university and with David Clemetson, he had also attended university and was an extremely wealthy individual.

It has to be said that not everybody in the British Colonies was in agreement that they should become embroiled in a war that wasn't of their making. Some elements of society were against sending their much needed supplies and money to Britain, when their own people were struggling to make do, and who generally were nowhere near as well off as their British cousins. It was hard for some to accept their own politicians' decision making process, who were apparently more concerned in appeasing the British Government than they were looking after the more vulnerable and less well off of their own communities. Add to the equation that the British authorities did not want black men joining the Army, and the only reason that they changed their stance on the issue was not because they wanted to but because they had to. By 1915 Britain and the other Allied nations were losing so many men who were either being killed or wounded, that they simply had no choice but to allow the formation of specific black units from the colonies to serve overseas in the different theatres of war. But even then, they did not want to pay them the same rate of pay as British soldiers.

Despite the politics and the arguments that were driving the issue of black men serving in the British Army, many of the young men from the islands of the West Indies found the prospect of joining the British Army a very appealing one. It meant a guaranteed wage, which in turn meant they could provide for their families, and the knowledge that they would be well fed. There was very little in the way of work for them back home and for those that did manage to find work, it was usually poorly paid.

Despite these particular issues, recruitment in the West Indies was hampered with what became known as the Halifax Incident. On 6 March 1916, the SS *Verdala* left Kingston in Jamaica en route to England, on board were 25 officers and 1,115 men from the other ranks. They were all members of the British West Indies Regiment. A short while in to the journey the *Verdala* was re-directed to the port of Halifax in Nova Scotia because of the potential threat of attack by German submarines. The change of direction resulted in the *Verdala* not coming into contact with any U-Boats who were actively searching the high seas for potential targets, but it also took them straight in to the path of a devastating blizzard.

A combination of poor heating on board the vessel and the soldiers having been issued with insufficient warm clothing, was a disaster waiting to happen. By the time the *Verdala* reached Halifax, 600 men were suffering with exposure and frostbite, five of whom died, and 106 were in such a bad state that they were admitted to hospital, with 100 of them subsequently having to have limbs amputated. It is not known where the five men who died are buried.

One of those on board the *Verdala* was **John Albert Edward Robertson Daley**, who was born on 5 February 1898 in Jamaica. On 19 January 1916, he enlisted in the British West Indies Regiment, and was posted to the 2nd (Jamaica) Battalion. He was confirmed in the rank of temporary second lieutenant on the day that the *Verdala* departed Kingston, Jamaica.

After arriving in England he transferred to No.13 Squadron of the Royal Flying Corps, where on 6 April 1917, he became a flying officer. He later transferred to No.24 Squadron where he shot down five enemy aircraft and two observation kite balloons, in the five months from March to July 1918. For these feats he was awarded the Distinguished Flying Cross, but sadly he was killed in action on 8 July 1918, just a week after his final 'kill'.

The citation for the award of his Distinguished Flying Cross appeared in the *London Gazette* on 3 August 1918.

> *'This officer has destroyed five enemy aeroplanes and two kite balloons, displaying marked skill and daring in these several actions, and also in attacking troops close to the ground.'*

At the time of his death, John was still only 20 years of age. He is buried in the British Cemetery at the village of Fienvillers, in the Somme region of France. The 34th and 38th Casualty Clearing Stations had been located at Fienvillers from May 1918.

Chapter Eight

23rd (Service) Battalion, (2nd Football) Middlesex Regiment (Duke of Cambridge's Own)

During the First World War a total of 559 officers and men from the 23rd Battalion, Middlesex Regiment (Duke of Cambridge's Own), including Walter Tull, were killed. The first member of the battalion to be killed during the First World War was Private (L/6124) Reginald **Allgrove**, who died on 18/06/1916. He is buried at the Tancrez Farm Cemetery, which is south of Ypres and which during the First World War was a British and Allied first aid post.

The names of these men are recorded in the date order of when they died.

Private (16124) R. **Allgrove**. Died 18/06/1916.

Private (1420) L. **Janson**. Died 19/06/1916.

Lance Corporal (3196) W.C. **Costa**. Died 20/06/1916.

Private (883) H.H. **Bench**. Died 23/06/1916.

Private (1675) E. **Quilter**. Died 24/06/1916.

Private (2261) Frederick Ernest **Smith**. Died 03/07/1916.

Private (3065) A.J. **Simms**. Died 04/07/1916.

Lance Serjeant (2164) H. **Ford**. Died 06/07/1916.

Private (9283) George **Collier**. Died 07/07/1916.

Private (3264) H.C. **McClellan**. Died 07/07/1916.

Lance Corporal (1925) H.H. **Prestidge**. Died 07/07/1916.

Private (2380) W.H. **Tudor**. Died 07/07/1916.

Private (F/2313) George **Snell**. Died 11/07/1916.

Private (F/174) L. **West**. Died 11/07/1916.

Private (1843) William Alfred **Leach**. Died 13/07/1916.

Private (L/16122) W.A. **Elmes**. Died 24/07/1916.

Private (G/11371) W.A. **Greenway**. Died 24/07/1916.

Private (3252) B.D. **Mann**. Died 27/07/1916.

Private (10337) H. **Mumbray**. Died 27/07/1916.

Private (2292) P.A. **White**. Died 27/07/1916.

Private (F/1881) C.V. **Ward**. Died 27/07/1916.

Serjeant (L/13687) S.E. **Bottom**. Died 31/07/1916.

Private (3119) A. **Foster**. Died 01/08/1916.

Private (F/2193) Francis James **Humphries**. Died 05/08/1916.

Private (493) Stephen **Cummings**. Died 13/08/1916.

Private (2355) H. **Lawley**. Died 13/08/1916.

Private (2234) G.A. **Brewster**. Died 15/08/1916.

Private (2309) B. **Smith**. Died 16/08/1916.

Private (F/1962) Joseph **Harvey**. Died 11/09/1916.

Private (F/3161) Edwin H. **Pile**. Died 11/09/1916.

Private (F/1967) Thomas **Bissell**. Died 12/09/1916.

Private (F/1716) F. **Cutler**. Died 12/09/1916.

Private (F/2247) Thomas W. **Brockington**. Died 12/09/1916.

Private (F/3126) Frank Stanley **Cooper**. Died 12/09/1916.

Private (F/2045) Francis William **Wotten**. Died 12/09/1916.

Private (F/3202) Richard **Gold**. Died 13/09/1916.

Corporal (PS/2597) Roy Herrick **Toplis**. Died 13/09/1916.

Private (G/11667) F.H.I. **Bliss**. Died 15/09/1916.

Private (F/1853) Job L. **Brown**. Died 15/09/1916.

Private (G/17909) Frederick C. **Burkett**. Died 15/09/1916.

Private (TF/2353) Robert H. **Crabtree**. Died 15/09/1916.

Corporal (F/2262) James H. **Davis**. Died 15/09/1916.

Private (G/5668) William E. **Demain**. Died 15/09/1916.

Private (G/11571) Charles E. **Everitt**. Died 15/09/1916.

Private (G/9748) Frank **Farmer**. Died 15/09/1916.

Private (F/2282) William James **Fletcher**. Died 15/09/1916.

Company Serjeant Major (F/1718) G. **Hamilton**. Died 15/09/1916.

Private (G/11490) William **Harris**. Died 15/09/1916.

Lance Corporal ((F/2364) Albert H. **Haughton**. Died 15/09/1916

Private (F/1635) Horace **Hind**. Died 15/09/1916.

Private (F/2392) Robert A. **Hedges**. Died 15/09/1916.

Private (G/20633) Arthur J. **Hoare**. Died 15/09/1916.

Private (F/2440) John **Holloway**. Died 15/09/1916.

Private (F/2785) Michael **Hornick**. Died 15/09/1916.

Private (F/2779) James **Howarth**. Died 15/09/1916.

Private (F/3168) Henry **Humphrey**. Died 15/09/1916.

Private (G/11605) James **Lapsley**. Died 15/09/1916.

Private (F/1887) Herbert J. **Laver**. Died 15/09/1916.

Private (G/2346) Tom **Mansell**. Died 15/09/1916.

Private (G/12446) Arthur G. **Marshall**. Died 15/09/1916.

Private (F/2768) John H. **Moore**. Died 15/09/1916.

Private (2361) Joseph **Neal**. Died 15/09/1916.

Second Lieutenant Lionel Phillip **Nixon**. Died 15/09/1916.

Private (F/2284) Henry **Parr**. Died 15/09/1916.

Private (F/3139) John **Piper**. Died 15/09/1916.

Private (F/2002) Joseph **Radford**. Died 15/09/1916.

Lance Corporal (F/1948) Ernest **Rickaby**. Died 15/09/1916.

Private (F/1818) James E. **Roberts**. Died 15/09/1916.

Private (G/17930) George **Sinclair**. Died 15/09/1916.

Private (G/10789) H. **Soward**. Died 15/09/1916.

Private (F/1233) Albert E. **Stopps**. Died 15/09/1916.

Private (F/2157) G.H. **Stopps**. Died 15/09/1916.

Private (G/11492) William **Wolfe**. Died 15/09/1916.

Lieutenant Francis **Wrentmore**. Died 16/09/1916.

Private (2414) Leonard **Edgecox**. Died 16/09/1916.

Private (2344) E.W. **Green**. Died 17/09/1916.

Lance Corporal (15994) Frank Stewart **Smithson**. Died 17/09/1916.

Private (11238) W. **Yardley**. Died 17/09/1916.

Private (G/11382) Leonard **Paddington**. Died 18/09/1916.

Private (1934) W. **Griggs**. Died 19/09/1916.

Private (2770) C.McL. **Moore**. Died 19/09/1916.

Private (11332) Ernest James **Cowdrey**. Died 21/09/1916.

Lance Corporal (G/13842) W. **Bysouth**. Died 22/09/1916.

Lance Corporal (11489) F.P. **Vickery**. Died 25/09/1916.

Private (3222) Bertie **Timms**. Died 26/09/1916.

Private (F/346) Louis Edward **Kennewell**. Died 28/09/1916.

Private (G/29565) George T. **Barton**. Died 01/10/1916.

Private (F/3239) Harold **Briggs**. Died 01/10/1916.

Private (F/2115) Alan Albert **Brockington**. Died 01/10/1916.

Private (G/11627) Henry J. **Bromley**. Died 01/10/1916.

Private (G/11308) William C. **Burt**. Died 01/10/1916.

Private (G/11418) Robert Harold M. **Caley**. Died 01/10/1916.

Private (F/1581) Ernest **Chesnaye**. Died 01/10/1916

Private (F/2158) William **Constance**. Died 01/10/1916.

Private (F/3033) William E. **Cook**. Died 01/10/1916.

Private (G/29426) Reginald Eric **Crooks**. Died 01/10/1916.

Private (F/2218) Albert H. **Deighton**. Died 01/10/1916.

Private (G/847) Henry **Elsom**. Died 01/10/1916.

Private (G/29625) W.H. **Green**. Died 01/10/1916.

Lance Serjeant (G/9394) Richard **Hoile**. Died 01/10/1916.

Private (G/29620) William G. **Marriott**. Died 01/10/1916.

Private (G/17815) Charles R. **Matthews**. Died 01/10/1916.

Private (G11341) Edward **Nash**. Died 01/10/1916.

Private (F/3118) Samuel **Neeves**. Died 01/10/1916.

Private (L/13019) William **Schumann**. Died 01/10/1916.

Private (G/11479) Mark **Stomoff**. Died 01/10/1916.

Serjeant (2034) C.T. **Gilkes**. Died 04/10/1916.

Private (F/1692) Henry A. **Hall**. Died 05/10/1916.

Private (G/20075) Walter **Attack**. Died 10/10/1916.

Lance Corporal (F/164) Charles Edward **Begent**. Died 10/10/1916.

Private (G/11600) Patrick **Harold**. Died 10/10/1916.

Serjeant (F/2407) John **Casey**. Died 11/10/1916.

Private (G/14384) Joseph P. **Haughey**. Died 11/10/1916.

Lance Corporal (F/1336) Albert Edward **Griffin**. Died 21/10/1916.

Lance Corporal (F/2416) J.G. **Strong**. Died 26/10/1916.

Private (29939) F. **Unwin**. Died 17/11/1916.

Private (G/11296) William Henry **Simmonds**. Died 01/12/1916.

Private (6053) B.A. **Hill**. Died 07/12/1916.

Private (G/11576) Alfred **Jones**. Died 15/12/1916.

Private (29920) G.A. **Stone**. Died 21/01/1917.

Private (G/11589) Archibald **Fordham**. Died 28/01/1917.

Private (G/11576) William Henry **Harmes**. Died 28/01/1917.

Private (13721) Walter Sidney **Garrard**. Died 29/01/1917.

Private (2015) Victor John **Gingell**. Died 29/01/1917.

Second Lieutenant Norman C.A. **Negretti**. Died 30/01/2017.

Private (2107) H. **Canning**. Died 01/02/1917.

Private (2829) William Henry **Feakins**. Died 03/02/1917.

Lance Corporal (2399) George Henry **Stevens**. Died 11/02/1917.

Private (11577) J. **Boddington**. Died 20/02/1917.

Second Lieutenant Albert **Bedingham**. Died 25/02/1917.

Private (24304) William Arthur **Curtis**. Died 21/03/1917.

Second Lieutenant Francis **Gore**. Died 26/03/1917.

Private (2706) William George **Campling**. Died 02/04/1917.

Private (F/3390) Arthur Pangbourne **Hawkins**. Died 02/04/1917

Private (G/9643) Frederick John **Lee**. Died 03/04/1917.

Private (2314) Henry Charles **Collins**. Died 11/04/1917.

Second Lieutenant Howard Wrey **Hanby**. Died 30/04/1917.

Private (15318) H.A. **Banfield**. Died 04/05/1917.

Private (F/2676) James **Lower**. Died 09/05/1917.

Private (3268) Frederick Frank **Neave**. Died 20/05/1917.

Private (8632) G. **Boltwood**. Died 27/05/1917.

Serjeant (9751) J. **Lovegrove**. Died 27/05/1917.

Private (24833) P.A. **Ledger**. Died 28/05/1917.

Serjeant (2457) James **Redfearn**. Died 28/05/1917.

Private (2252) John Oliver **Spencer**. Died 28/05/1917.

Private (24819) S.C. **Taafe**. Died 28/05/1917.

Private (G/28160) Ernest Richard **Hailey**. Died 01/06/1917.

Private (F/3030) Herbert **Ackroyd**. 07/06/1917.

Private (G/19721) George **Anscombe**. Died 07/06/1917.

Private (11421) Robert **Archer**. Died 07/06/1917.

Private (G/51001) Richard **Barnes**. Died 07/06/1917.

Private (G/14082) William **Batt**. Died 07/06/1917.

Private (G/9047) Alfred **Camm**. Died 07/06/1917.

Private (F/1808) Arthur E. **Clarke**. Died 07/06/1917.

Private (G/193) W. **Collins**. Died 07/06/1917.

Private (TF/203036) William G. **Constable**. Died 07/06/1917.

Lance Corporal (F/1946) Frank **Donnelly**. Died 07/06/1917.

Private (G/34508) John A. **Freeman**. Died 07/06/1917.

Corporal (G/44168) Harry Noel **Gamble**. Died 07/06/1917.

Private (F/3323) Rupert E. **Goble**. Died 07/06/1917.

Private (F/1982) Frank **Hack**. Died 07/06/1917.

Private (G/22809) W.T.C. **Hewitt**. Died 07/06/1917.

Private (G/20239) Arnold **Inglesby**. Died 07/06/1917.

Private (F/3027) W. **Johnson**. Died 07/06/1917.

Private (G/24888) Albert B. **Kent**. Died 07/06/1917.

Private (G/12444) Alfred T. **King**. Died 07/06/1917.

Private (G/20059) Fred **Linnell**. Died 07/06/1917.

Second Lieutenant James Beaton **McKinnon**. Died 07/06/1917.

Private (TF/204497) Robert **Mills**. Died 07/06/1917.

Captain Frederick **Norris**. Died 07/06/1917.

Private (TF/023384) Edward G. **Pedder**. Died 07/06/1917.

Lance Corporal (2092) E. **Pickering**. Died 07/06/1917.

Lieutenant Thomas Warren **Purves**. Died 07/06/1917.

Private (33416) John **Riley**. Died 07/06/1917.

Private (G/24901) Charles **Rumsey**. Died 07/06/1917.

Private (F/2304) Harold F. **Snape**. Died 07/06/1917.

Private (F/1546) William F. **Stevens**. Died 07/06/1917.

Lance Corporal (F/168) Frederick **Stringer**. Died 07/06/1917.

Private (G/50984) Harry **Thornycroft**. Died 07/06/1917.

Private (SR/7191) Herbert **Trott**. Died 07/06/1917.

Private (F/1542) George H. **Wensley**. Died 07/06/1917.

Lance Corporal (G/13012) Richard Henry Edward **Wilson**. Died 07/06/1917.

Private (24894) Albert W.G. **Whittington**. Died 07/06/1917.

Private (2578) W.J. **Savidge**. Died 08/06/1917.

Private (1410) Eric Stanley **Francis**. Died 09/06/1917.

Private (G/8327) Albert Thompson **Clay**. 11/06/1917.

Private (L/14940) Ernest W. **Say**. Died 11/06/1917.

Private (2038) Albert **Shore**. Died 15/06/1917.

Lance Corporal (32632) W. **Stone**. Died 16/06/1917.

Private (G/11574) Frank **Barnett**. Died 17/06/1917.

Private (F/1469) L. **Hand**. Died 18/06/1917.

Private (F/3232) William Samuel **Vines**. Died 19/06/1917.

Private (G/11272) George **Chevert**. Died 21/06/1917.

Lance Corporal (F/2233) Walter F. **Cupper**. Died 21/06/1917.

Private (G/11413) Thomas **Grant**. Died 21/06/1917.

Private (SR/6767) George **Witts**. Died 21/06/1917.

Private (F/1244) Charles **Austin**. Died 22/06/1917.

Private (TF/203688) Albert **Dodd**. Died 22/06/1917.

Private (G/10778) William H.T. **Holmes**. Died 22/06/1917.

Private (G/19615) Charles **Parrott**. Died 22/06/1917.

Lance Corporal (2001) Albert Victor **Bolshaw**. Died 25/06/1917

Private (2231) S. **Buss**. Died 25/06/1917.

Private (2302) Francis Edgar **Gibbs** MM. Died 25/06/1917.

Private (17821) W.J. **Hyde**. Died 25/06/1917.

Corporal (21637) Howard George **Wright**. Died 25/06/1917.

Private (2245) E. **Potts** MM. Died 26/06/1917.

Private (3153) Francis Ralph **Wickenden**. Died 26/06/1917.

Private (27471) C. **Kemp**. Died 27/06/1917.

Private (2330) George **Kendall**. Died 27/06/1917.

Lance Serjeant (TF/235277) Harry **Lightoller**. Died 03/07/1917

Private (PW/5964) Albert E. **Hays**. Died 19/07/1917.

Private (TF/267259) John Alfred **Gartside**. Died 27/07/1917.

Private (TF/200689) William James **Thompson**. Died 27/07/1917.

Private (TF/206169) Phillip J. **Baker**. Died 31/07/1917.

Private (G/52222) Arthur **Bennison**. Died 31/07/1917.

Private (G/29424) George **Boisson**. Died 31/07/1917.

Private (G/29525) Robert **Brown**. Died 31/07/1917.

Private (G/52227) John Thomas **Coe**. Died 31/07/1917.

Private (2782) C.H. **Coles**. Died 31/07/1917.

Private (G/52233) James **Dawson**. Died 31/07/1917.

Private (G/24818) Victor C. **Day**. Died 31/07/1917.

Second Lieutenant Frederick Herbert **Devereux**. Died 31/07/1917.

Private (TF/206174) James H. **Ferris**. Died 31/07/1917.

Private (G/43611) Bertram **Foster**. Died 31/07/1917.

Private (F/2443) Arthur D. **Greaves**. Died 31/07/1917.

Private (G/89254) Henry **Jordan**. Died 31/07/1917.

Private (G/15575) Frederick **King**. Died 31/07/1917.

Private (G/28480) Dennis **Hillier**. Died 31/07/1917.

Private (G/5225) James A. **Holt**. Died 31/07/1917.

Private (G/24520) George A. **Howlett**. Died 31/07/1917.

Private (F/2769) Bruce R. **Moore**. Died 31/07/1917.

Private (G/20089) Albert Phillip **Nock**. Died 31/07/1917.

Lance Corporal (L/13403) Benjamin W. **Page**. Died 31/07/1917.

Private (SR/6522) Charles T. **Pearce**. Died 31/07/1917.

Lieutenant Neil **Shoobert**. Died 31/07/1917.

Private (G/52298) Reginald G. **Simpson**. Died 31/07/1917.

Private (G/5277) William **Stead**. Died 31/07/1917.

Second Lieutenant James Lindsay **Sutherland**. Died 31/07/1917.

Private (G/11663) Sidney **Taylor**. Died 31/07/1917.

Private (G/52291) John H. **Ward**. Died 31/07/1917.

Private (G/52288) Herbert Allen **Wardman**. Died 31/07/1917.

Private (F/1539) Albert **Wilson**. Died 31/07/1917.

Private (52234) R. **Hildreth**. Died 01/08/1917.

Lance Corporal (G/11588) George **Anscombe** Died 10/08/1917.

Private (6726) Albert George **Newman**. Died 10/08/1917.

Corporal (TF/235283) James F. **Popple**. Died 10/08/1917.

Corporal (F/1663) Gilbert **Williams**. Died 10/08/1917.

Lance Corporal (G/11588) Godfrey **Williams**. Died 10/08/1917.

Private (F/590) Burt Elvedine **Tyler**. Died 17/08/1917.

Private (G/11336) Ernest **Childs**. Died 21/08/1917.

Second Lieutenant William **Campbell**. Died 20/09/2017.

Second Lieutenant Krikor **Gulbenkian**. Died 20/09/1917.

Corporal (11559) Ernest Fredrick **Sprague**. Died 20/09/1917.

Corporal (G/2414) John E. **Clark**. Died 21/09/1917.

Lance Corporal (G/50158) Sidney W. **Mason**. Died 21/09/1917.

Private (TF/206179) Percival Edward **Rattue**. Died 21/09/1917.

Private (F/621) Edward **Scammell**. Died 21/09/1917.

Private (G/52280) Christopher **Sykes**. Died 21/09/1917.

Private (G/52209) John W. **Andrews**. Died 22/09/1917.

Lance Corporal (G/26812) Beaumont E. **Atkinson**. Died 22/09/1917.

Private (TF/204964) Frederick **Broderick**. Died 22/09/1917.

Private (F/2396) Percy James **Glover**. Died 22/09/1917.

Private (TF/202194) Horace **Lawson**. Died 22/09/1917.

Private (G/43364) Charles W.J. **Lince**. Died 22/09/1917.

Private (204400) O.E. **Osbourne**. Died 22/09/1917.

Private (G/40920) Reginald **Peck**. Died 22/09/1917.

Private (G/1426) James **Reed**. Died 22/09/1917.

Private (G/52278) Arthur **Sanderson**. Died 22/09/1917.

Private (PS/3558) Henry **Woollett**. Died 22/09/1917.

Private (G/52238) Frank **Goodall**. Died 23/09/1917.

Private (2403) A.E. **Byng**. Died 24/09/1917.

Private (204494) J. **Kent**. Died 24/09/1917.

Private (15497) J. **Brannan**. Died 29/10/1917.

Private (G/7850) Walter **Goddard**. Died 05/12/1917.

Private (G/4752) J.E. **Keary**. Died 04/03/1918.

Private (G/20747) Colin **Hall**. Died 22/03/1918.

Private (G/29574) H.G. **Hicks**. Died 22/03/1918.

Private (F/2042) A. **Madden**. Died 22/03/1918.

Private (TF/202713) Herbert **Roper**. Died 22/03/1918.

Private (F/465) W. **Rowsell**. Died 22/03/1918.

Private (F/2271) Thomas **Smith**. Died 22/03/1918.

Private (G/5737) William **Spendlove**. Died 22/03/1918.

Lance Corporal (G/24270) Albert C. **Coffee**. Died 23/03/1918.

Private (TF/265860) Frederick A. **Derrick**. Died 23/03/1918.

Private (G/41078) Albert **Edwards**. Died 23/03/1918.

Lance Corporal (TF/235361) Charles **Foord**. Died 23/03/1918.

Lance Corporal (TF/200381) Joseph W. **Harris**. Died 23/03/1918.

Private (44239) A. **Hope**. Died 23/03/1918.

Private (TF/242135) Jamie **Huber**. Died 23/03/1918.

Serjeant (PS/2335) Archibald L. **Hurley**. Died 23/03/1918.

Private (PS/3543) H. **Poore**. Died 23/03/1918.

Private (TF/201662) Charles W. **Archer**. Died 24/03/1918.

Private (G/21164) Edwin H. **Bateman**. Died 24/03/1918.

Private (G/52228) Stanley **Collinson**. Died 24/03/1918.

Private (TF/242170) William E. **Cozens**. Died 24/03/1918.

Private (G/20878) Harold F. **Cracknell**. Died 24/03/1918.

Lance Corporal (F/1902) B. **Cross**. Died 24/03/1918.

Private (G/89620) Frederick J. **Donaldson**. Died 24/03/1918.

Private (G/50009) Edward **Dumbrell**. Died 24/03/1918.

Private (TF/242177) John F. **Fish**. Died 24/03/1918.

Private (G/43343) Leonard W. **Fludder**. Died 24/03/1918.

Private (G/52236) Michael **Forkin**. Died 24/03/1918.

Private (TF/235299) James **Garbett**. Died 24/03/1918.

Private (11518) James **Geeham**. Died 24/03/1918.

Private (G/60314) Leslie C **Hughes**. Died 24/03/1918.

Corporal (G/11303) Albert Edwin **Ison**. Died 24/03/1918.

Private (G/29002) Bertie D. **May**. Died 24/03/1918.

Private (G/11359) Charles **McElligot**. Died 24/03/1918.

Lance Corporal (G/52271) John W. **Readman**. Died 24/03/1918

Private (G/41353) Alfred J. **Sawyer**. Died 24/03/1918.

Private (G/60398) Charles E. **Speck**. Died 24/03/1918.

Private (L/15808) Francis Joseph **Versey**. Died 24/03/1918.

Private (TF/242152) Albert A. **Wright**. Died 24/03/1918.

Private (L/17114) Horace S. **Yeulett**. Died 24/03/1918.

Private (F/2197) James **Allen**. Died 25/03/1918.

Private (F/3112) Henry James **Andrews**. Died 25/03/1918.

Private (G/19766) George W. **Baston**. Died 25/03/1918.

Lance Corporal (G/28215) John C. **Clarke**. Died 25/03/1918.

Private (G/44233) Cyril **Danby**. Died 25/03/1918.

Private (L/16525) T.S.C. **Dent**. Died 25/03/1918.

Private (G/12683) Jack **Diamondstone**. Died 25/03/1918.

Private (G/40509) Lionel Maurice **Fryer**. Died 25/03/1918.

Private (G/13764) Alfred **Gater**. Died 25/03/1918.

Private (TF/235300) Fred **Genders**. Died 25/03/1918.

Lieutenant Colonel Alan Roderick **Haig-Brown**. Died 25/03/1918

Private (G/20186) Bertie J. **Harris**. Died 25/03/1918.

Private (G/52297) Horner M. **Walker**. Died 25/03/1918.

Private (G/11494) Henry John **King**. Died 25/03/1918.

Private (G/86395) William R. **Lowe**. Died 25/03/1918.

Private (G/42318) Fran **Pocock**. Died 25/03/1918.

Private (G/52270) Harold **Poppleton**. Died 25/03/1918.

Private (G/42731) Percy E. **Relf**. Died 25/03/1918.

Private (TF/241643) William C. **Simmins**. Died 25/03/1918.

Lance Corporal (TF/241241) Lenox J. **Sirett**. Died 25/03/1918.

Private (TF/206156) William J. **Stringer**. Died 25/03/1916.

Private (G/25234) Alfred F. **Thomas**. Died 25/03/1918.

Private (G/40927) William J. **Timms**. Died 25/03/1918.

Second Lieutenant Walter Daniel John **Tull**. Died 25/03/1918.

Private (F/1282) J.H. **Jones**. Died 26/03/1918.

Lance Corporal (9978) S. **Thurbon**. Died 26/03/1918.

Lance Corporal (G/11419) John Joseph **Quick**. Died 26/03/1918.

Private (60686) S.E. **Nash**. Died 30/03/1918.

Private (242874) Arthur **Everhill**. Died 03/04/1918.

Private (52252) Henry Whalley **Heslop**. Died 03/04/1918.

Corporal (2006) Albert **Ames**. Died 06/04/1918.

Private (PS/2890) Walter Avery **Pontin**. Died 12/04/1918.

Serjeant (PW/6859) Albert J. **Farrow**. Died 14/04/1918.

Private (G/54570) Percy Henry **Bryant**. Died 19/04/1918.

Private (G/54570) Henry C. **Bryant**. Died 19/04/1918.

Private (54036) Alec Fred **Stephens**. Died 30/04/1918.

Private (G/50683) A. **Mileham**. Died 06/05/1918.

Private (50548) W.C. **Coast**. Died 08/05/1918.

Lance Corporal (G/50925) William E. **Peake**. Died 09/05/1918.

Private (G/72684) Ernest **Raggett**. Died 09/05/1918.

Private (203990) J. **Robinson**. Died 13/05/1918.

Private (242075) Walter **Wolfe**. Died 16/05/1918.

Private (41206) Albert J. **Harwood**. Died 18/05/1918.

Private (24850) M. **Gilding**. Died 24/05/1918.

Private (11319) Robert George **Gedge**. Died 25/05/1918.

Private (60483) C.H. **Goody**. Died 25/05/1918.

Private (60662) George Ernest **Rippingale**. Died 31/05/1918.

Private (F/901) Harold Stanley **Slade**. Died 31/05/1918.

Lance Corporal (20180) H.J. **Richardson**. Died 03/06/1918.

Private (13502) J.F. **Steward**. Died 08/07/1918.

Private (G/11643) T. **Ashley**. Died 15/07/1918.

Private (F/3149) Charles Adrian **Thatcher**. Died 20/07/1918.

Private (G/41180) Harry **Webb**. Died 22/07/1918.

Lance Serjeant (241239) A. **Gandy**. Died 09/08/1918.

Private (54605) John Alexander **Holmes**. Died 09/08/1918.

Private (71766) P.J. **Kitchener**. Died 19/08/1918.

Private (54582) J.J. **Easter**. Died 20/08/1918.

Private (54588) Thomas **Gray**. Died 20/08/1918.

Private (G/54619) Mark E. **Knight**. Died 20/08/1918.

Private (F/3237) William James **McNaught**. Died 20/08/1918.

Private (2118) A. **Tibbitts**. Died 20/08/1918.

Private (315498) Harry **Beck**. Died 22/09/1918.

Private (95046) J. **Dindus**. Died 22/08/1918.

Private (TF/204694) Louis Brereton **Jones**. Died 22/08/1918.

Private (54097) William Arthur **Deane**. Died 07/09/1918.

Private (60660) A. **Quibell**. Died 08/09/1918.

Private (52251) Albert Ernest **Hawkins**. Died 09/09/1918.

Private (G/52225) R. **Craggy**. Died 15/09/1918.

Private (G/54572) Gordon Crossley **Carter**. Died 29/09/1918.

Private (TF/204532) Dan **Allen**. Died 29/09/1918.

Private (G/54066) Ernest T. **Briggs**. Died 29/09/1918.

Private (F/2244) Harry **Cartwright**. Died 29/09/1918

Private (G/54521) James **Chandler**. Died 29/09/1918.

Private (G/60618) Frederick **Cook**. Died 29/09/1918.

Private (TF/203830) George E. **Cooper**. Died 29/09/1918.

Private (L/17394) Albert E. **Gadd**. Died 29/09/1918.

Lance Corporal (T/204666) Percy John **German**. Died 29/09/1918.

Private (TE/201217) Alfred **Hemmings**. Died 29/09/1918.

Private (G/54567) Ernest John **Mansell**. Died 29/09/1918.

Lance Corporal (G/636) James J. **Perry**. Died 29/09/1918.

Private (203590) Albert William **Randall**. Died 29/09/1918.

Private (G/54551) Ernest **Rolfe**. Died 29/09/1918.

Private (G/1871) Richard **Snell**. Died 29/09/1918.

Private (G/54047) William **Stephens**. Died 29/09/1918.

Private (G/60223) Harry Douglas **Stone**. Died 29/09/1918.

Private (F/2835) Richard E. **Taylor**. Died 29/09/1918.

Private (G/40223) F. **Taylor**. Died 29/09/1918.

Private (15415) S. **Thomas**. Died 29 /09/1918.

Private (G/54049) Ernest F. **Wild**. Died 29/09/1918.

Lance Corporal (G/87318) Harry Cecil **Carter**. Died 30/09/1918

Private (54573) F. **Currlin**. Died 30/09/1918.

Lance Corporal (G/40320) H.H. **Harmer**. Died 30/09/1918.

Lance Corporal (G/60588) Frederick Walter **Thew**. Died 30/09/1918.

Private (241184) Thomas **Ballard**. Died 01/10/1918.

Private (TF/204542) John **Clarke**. Died 01/10/1918.

Private (24304) T. **Cole**. Died 01/10/1918.

Private (2369) H. **Goulding**. Died 01/10/1918.

Private (206153) P.S. **Young**. Died 01/10/1918.

Private (204541) W.S. **Canning**. Died 02/10/1918.

Private (54656) James Herbert **Hopkins**. Died 02/10/1918.

Private (60665) Harry **Robinson**. Died 02/10/1918.

Private Andrew **Snowden**. Died 02/10/1918

Private (G/10497) Thomas F. **Taylor**. Died 02/10/1918.

Corporal (G/50131) Bert **Penney**. Died 03/10/1918.

Private (TF/241083) William Charles **Witts**. Died 03/10/1918.

Private (G/54072) F.A. **Beanlands**. Died 13/10/1918.

Private (3066) A. **Carroll**. Died 16/10/1918.

Lance Corporal (G/20415) J. **Weir**. Died 16/10/1918.

Private (54138) R.E.J. **Woolmore**. Died 17/10/1918.

Corporal (2236) George Henry **Hill** MM+Bar. Died 18/10/1918

Private (54044) C.F. **Turner**. Died 18/10/1918.

Serjeant (235274) G. **Warren**. Died 18/10/1918.

Lance Corporal (1741) Arthur **Plummer**. Died 21/10/1918.

Private (G/19792) William **Button**. Died 23/10/1918.

Private (316210) Harold **Morgan**. Died 23/10/1918.

Private (G/7740) Albert W. **Wells**. Died 23/10/1918.

Private (54612) F. **Lovegrove**. Died 24/10/1918.

Private (G/87361) Frank **Vickerstaff**. Died 24/10/1918.

Private (95370) Alfred **Dance**. Died 25/10/1918.

Private (G/54552) Arthur J. **Gardiner**. Died 25/10/1918.

Private (95380) R.S. **Rumbold**. Died 25/10/1918.

Serjeant (13833) W.H. **Callow**. Died 27/10/1918.

Private (G/89071) J.C. **Robinson**. Died 27/10/1918.

Private (1929) Frederick George **Day**. Died 05/11/1918.

Private (60695) W. **Ede**. Died 05/11/1918.

Post War Deaths

Private (L/12364) A. **Walker**. Died 10/02/1919.

Private (97019) Spencer Tate **Turner**. Died 06/12/1919.

Private (19289) Thomas **Harris**. Died 02/03/1920.

Private (G/42730) T.W.E. **Ford**. Died 23/08/1920.

Private (22164) Ernest William **Levy**. Died 13/03/1921.

An interesting fact to come out of this was that one of the 23rd Battalion's lieutenants, was 26-year-old Krikor Gulbenkian, who was killed on 20 September 1917 during the third Battle of Ypres, which took place between 31 July 1917 and 6 November 1917. He has no known grave and his name is commemorated on the Tyne Cot Memorial.

Krikor was born in London in 1891, but his father, Garabed, was born in Turkey, becoming a naturalised British subject in 1903. At the time of the First World War Turkey was part of the Ottoman Empire, so besides being an enemy nation, it could also be argued that Turkey was not a member state of Europe at the time, which if accepted, meant that under British military law of the time, Krikor should not have been allowed to become a British Army officer, as he wasn't of 'pure European descent'.

Sadly, the War Dairies for the 23rd Battalion, Middlesex Regiment were poorly kept, in that there was very little detailed information recorded in them. The entry for 18 June 1916 simply shows that the battalion were in trenches at Le Touquet and records the following, '*Casualties; killed other ranks, 1, wounded other ranks, 1.*' That's it. There is no mention of an incident explaining how one man was killed and another was wounded. The casualties are not even named; they are simply referred to as 'ORs', other ranks. The only individuals who were felt worthy enough to have their names mentioned in regimental war diaries, were officers.

Chapter Nine

Walter Tull's Army Service Record

Walter Tull's Army Service Record is preserved at the National Archive at Kew in West London. It is sixty-seven pages long and details his Army career from start to finish.

We will look at it in as much detail as possible to see if it throws up anything new about Walter that either hadn't previously been known about him, or that had simply been missed. It may also clear up the issue concerning whether or not he was ever recommended for the Military Cross.

The first thing that it shows is that a gratuity payment, under articles 496 and 497 of the Army Act, which was made in lieu of Walter's death totalling £73 1s 9d, was made to his next of kin, his brother, Edward Tull-Warnock, whose home address was 419 St Vincent Street, Glasgow.

The first pages of his Army Service Record, do not in fact contain too much in the way of relevant information, they are in the main minute sheets, which have a few lines of typed and handwritten comments and basic information, such as 'KILLED IN ACTION 25 March 1918'. The hand-written information is either in pencil, or blue and red ink.

Pages eleven and fourteen contain the same information, with the entry centred around what Walter's rank had been when he was discharged from the Army to be commissioned as an officer. It is a question sent in the form of a memo by The Secretary, War Office, Imperial Institute, South Kensington, London SW7, and is dated 15 December 1919.

'With reference to the estate of the late 2/Lieut. W D Tull, Middlesex Regiment, the Secretary of the War Office requests that you will be good enough to return this letter as early as possible, to the above

address, with a statement in the margin showing whether the late
officer held the rank of Lance-Sergt. or Sergeant at the time of his
discharge to a Commission.
   He was formerly No.55, 23rd Batt. Middlesex Regt.

   Please reply by return of post.
   Mark "Very Urgent"'

The enquiry had been sent to the Officer in Charge, No.1 Infantry
Records, Hanwell Park Schools, Hanwell. The reason why the question
was asked was because it would ultimately affect how much the final
amount of gratuity that would be paid to Walter's brother Edward.

   The memo was received by the Records Office on 18 December 1919
and their reply to the Secretary of the War Office was succinct. *'According*
to the records of this office, Lance Sergeant was the rank held on discharge.'

   Their reply is dated 31 December 1919 and was received at the War
Office on 3 January 1920.

   Page thirteen is a minute sheet concerning his commission as an officer. The stamp at the top of the page is that of the WAR OFFICE and is
dated 13 February 1917. Handwritten in blue ink at the top of the form,
it reads as follows: *'No.55 L/Sgt. Walter Daniel Tull 23rd Battn. Middlesex*
Regt.'

   There is then a small typed sentence which indicates that the named
individual, in this case Walter Tull, had been nominated for appointment
to a commission; then a space where the name of the regiment that the
individual is going to be commissioned into, but in Walter's case the name
of a regiment has not been entered. It states he had been accepted for
admission to No.10 Officer Cadet Battalion, and that he will join them
at Gailes in Scotland. Originally the course was due to have commenced
on 26 January 1917, but that date, which was typed, has been crossed
through in blue ink and then the date of 6 February 1917 has been hand-
written, also in blue ink.

Underneath this is a stamp mark which says, 'SEE LONDON GAZETTE 16 JUN 1917, SPECIAL RESERVE'.

Page seventeen, which being Walter's actual application for a commission to the rank of officer, would appear to be slightly out of place in the chronological order of the record. It is a form MT 392 and has to be completed by any candidate who, like Walter, was serving in the ranks of the New Armies, Special Reserve, or with the Territorial Force. Just to clarify, the application was for a temporary commission in the regular British Army for the duration of the war. Besides the usual information one would be expected to complete on such an application, such as name, address and date of birth, it also consisted of a total of fourteen questions. Some of Walter's answers to these questions were very interesting. Number four asked, 'Whether of pure European descent?' Walter's answer was, 'No', clarifying that the authorities knew that even though Walter was black and born in England, they now also knew, if they hadn't done so before, that he was not of pure European descent. He also clarified that he could not ride a horse, which was question number ten on the form.

His home address at the time was recorded as being that of his brother Edward, who lived at 419 St Vincent Street, Glasgow.

Question thirteen enquired as to which branch of the service an applicant would be desirous of serving in. Walter answered that he was willing to serve in either the, 'Infantry, or the Wireless Equipment Department of the Royal Flying Corps' and in answer to which specific unit he would like to be appointed to, he replied either '17th Battalion, Middlesex Regiment or the Royal Flying Corps'. This section of the form is dated 25 November 1916.

The form had to be countersigned by an individual of 'position' who could confirm that they had known Walter for at least four years and that he was of 'good moral character'. Walter opted to have his solicitor in Northampton countersign the form for him. It also had to be signed by someone who could confirm that he had 'attained a good standard of education'. For this, Walter had turned to, Mr Stimpson the chief assistant headteacher from the Avenue School in Northampton.

As Walter was serving in the ranks at the time of his application, he needed it to be approved and signed by his commanding officer. In this case it was Lieutenant Colonel Alan Roderick Haig-Brown, commanding officer of the 23rd Battalion, Middlesex Regiment, who happily agreed to sign the recommendation for Walter's appointment as a temporary commission in the Regular Army, a rank that was held for the duration of the war.

Walter's Attestation document for when he enlisted as a private soldier, is not at the beginning of his Army Service Record, but is included on page twenty-four. He signed up on 21 December 1914 at Kingsway in London, becoming Private (55) in the 17th (1st Football) Battalion, Middlesex Regiment. He was 26 years of age and living at 33 Albany Road, Northampton, and his occupation was recorded as being a professional footballer. The following is a list of his different postings and appointments before he was commissioned as an officer.

21/12/14 – Attested – Private – 17th Battalion.
12/02/15 – Appointed unpaid – Lance Corporal – 17th Battalion.
12/02/15 – Appointed paid – Lance Corporal – 17th Battalion.
04/05/15 – Promoted – Corporal – 17th Battalion.
05/07/15 – Appointed paid – Lance Serjeant – 17th Battalion.
10/05/16 – Posted – Lance Serjeant – Depot.
08/08/16 – Posted – Lance Serjeant – 27th Battalion.
01/09/16 – Posted – Lance Serjeant – 6th Battalion.
14/09/16 – Appointed paid – L/Sgt – 6th Battalion.
20/09/16 – Posted – Lance Serjeant – BEF Depot.
20/09/16 – Posted – Lance Serjeant – 23rd Battalion.
26/12/16 – Posted – Lance Serjeant – Depot.
29/05/17 – Discharged under para 392 (xixa), King's Regulations, for the benefit of the public service for the purpose of being appointed to a Commission. His time in the Army in the other ranks was spent accordingly.
Home: 21/12/14 – 16/11/15.
British Expeditionary Force, France: 17/11/15 – 09/05/16

Home: 10/05/16 – 19/09/16
British Expeditionary Force, France: 20/09/16 – 25/12/16
Home: 26/12/16 – 29/05/17

He had served for a total of two years 160 days. Notification of his Commission appeared in the edition of the *London Gazette* dated 16 June 1917.

Walter's casualty sheet whilst on active service shows that on 27 April 1916, the day before his twenty-eighth birthday, he was admitted to the 6th Field Ambulance, of the Royal Army Medical Corps, and treated for what has been recorded as 'acute mania'. This more than likely means shell-shock, but that term wasn't coined until 1917 by a medical officer called Charles Myers, and the term didn't just relate to men who had been exposed to exploding shells, it was also about men having to endure long periods of fighting, living on the edge as well as possessing feelings of fear and emotion. In Walter's case, for the seven months prior to his diagnosis he had been in France without leave, the last nine days of which he had spent in the front line trenches without rest, enduring extensive bombardments, whilst witnessing men dying all around him, and trying to stay strong and lead his men as an officer was expected to do.

Because of the severity of his condition he was admitted to No.8 Stationary Hospital at Wimereux the next day, and later the same day he was transferred to No.7 General Hospital which at the time was situated at St Omer. With no sign of any improvement in his condition, the decision was taken that he should be sent back to England for further treatment. He was sent home on board His Majesty's Hospital Ship *St Denis* on 9 May 1916.

Acute mania or shell-shock as it was eventually called, was a totally new phenomenon for doctors to have to deal with; not only was there no definitive understanding of exactly what caused the condition, but neither was it clear how to best treat it. By the end of the war more than 80,000 cases of shell-shock had been dealt with by British Army medical units.

Some senior officers saw shell-shock as nothing more than weakness, or an excuse for cowardice. Some men suffering with the condition were charged with the offence of cowardice and some of those men who were convicted were even executed by firing squad.

Walter arrived back in France on 20 September 1916, joined the depot and was taken on the strength of the 23rd Battalion. After a month's acclimatisation training, he re-joined his battalion in the field on 29 October 1916, before returning to England just two months later on 25 December to commence his officer training.

Towards the end of his service record is a copy of the telegram sent by the Secretary of the War Office, to Walter's brother Edward, at his home address of 419 St Vincent Street, Glasgow. It is dated 4 April 1918, ten days after Walter Tull was killed in action. The telegram informing Edward of his brother's death, consists of four lines.

'*Deeply regret 2/Lieut W D Tull, Middlesex Regiment, killed in action March twenty-fifth. The Army Council express sympathy.*'

Walter's Army Service Record did not include any mention of his having been recommended for the award of the Military Cross, but nor did it indicate anywhere that he had been Mentioned in Despatches.

The last item was quite poignant – a letter written by the War Office and which had been posted to Walter's brother Edward, outlining what they did and didn't know about the circumstances surrounding his death. It was an apparent response to a letter that Edward had written in enquiring about how Walter had died. It is a typewritten letter and is dated 12 April 1918.

'*The Military Secretary presents his compliments to Mr Tull-Warnock, and, in reply to his letter of the 9th instant, begs to inform him that no details respecting the death of 2nd Lieutenant W D Tull, 5th att. 23rd Middlesex Regiment, have been received at the War Office, the names of officers who have been killed in action being*' *only rendered on a list sent to the War Office by the Base or General Headquarters in the Field.*

The Military Secretary begs to suggest that Mr Tull-Warnock should write to:-

The Officer Commanding
23rd Middlesex Regiment
British Expeditionary Force,

who is the only person in a position to furnish any details, and who, when he can find time, it is felt sure, would be only too glad to supply any information which he may have in his possession.

The Military Secretary begs to say that Commanding Officers, when out of the Line, generally do write to relatives of Officers who have fallen, though it is not part of their official duties to do so; but in times of great stress and heavy fighting, as Mr Tull-Warnock will readily understand, their time is primarily taken up with their arduous battle duties etc., and that very often there must inevitably be some delay in writing or in answering any letters they may receive.

The portion of Mr Tull-Warnock's letter respecting the place of burial and the personal effects of the late 2nd Lieutenant Tull has been passed to the department concerned, from whom he will no doubt hear in due course.

The Military Secretary is desired by the Secretary of State for War to express his deepest sympathy with Mr Tull-Warnock in the loss of his gallant brother.'

One can only hope that the German soldiers who discovered Walter Tull's body lying in no man's land, having recently despatched him from this world, did the decent thing and buried him the best way that they could, along with the other members of the Middlesex Regiment who fell in battle that day. In Walter's case, it most definitely is a case of, 'gone but definitely not forgotten'.

Chapter Ten

War Memorials

More than one memorial commemorates the name of Walter Tull. His is one of the names inscribed on the **Arras Memorial** in the Pas de Calais region of France. It carries the names of 34,765 men from the United Kingdom, New Zealand and South Africa, who died in the region between April 1916 and 7 August 1918 and who have no known grave.

In the case of Walter Tull, his body was seen by his men, in fact some of them tried to retrieve it immediately after he was shot, but were prevented from doing so by heavy German machine-gun fire. They were left with no option but to withdraw without him, so as to prevent what would have been the senseless loss of their own lives. Once the fighting had stopped, it is hoped that German soldiers would have retrieved his body and those of his comrades and provided them with a Christian burial, and not just left them in no man's land. There were ninety other men besides Walter from the Middlesex Regiment who died on 25 March 1918, fifty-nine of whom have no known grave and their names are commemorated on either the Arras or Pozières memorials. It is almost inconceivable to believe that the bodies of these men would not have been gathered up and buried somewhere in a communal grave, and that in the confusion of war the location has simply been lost.

Canadian and Australian military personnel who were killed in the region, mainly during the Arras Offensive of April/May 1917, and the big German attack during the spring of 1918, have separate memorials at Vimy and Villers-Bretonneux.

There is the Walter Tull Memorial which sits on a green outside **Northampton Town Football Club,** which was erected by the club in 1999. The wording on one side of it is as follows:

'Through his actions W.D.J. Tull ridiculed the barriers of ignorance that were to deny people of colour equality with their contemporaries. His life stands testament to a determination to confront those people and those obstacles that sought to diminish him and the world in which he lived. It reveals a man though rendered breathless in his prime, whose strong heart still beats loudly. This memorial marks an area of reflective space as a garden of remembrance.'

The wording on the opposite side is:

'Walter Daniel John Tull
born 8 April 1888.
1909 – Tottenham Hotspur F.C.
1911 – Northampton Town F. C.
1914 – Enlisted in the 17th Battalion, 1st Football.
1917 – The first black Briton to be commissioned a combat officer.
1918 – He was killed at the second Battle of the Somme.
He was awarded the 1914 – 15 Star and British War and Victory medals.'

There is another memorial to Walter Tull outside the Sixfields stadium in Northampton. Its inscription is as follows:

'Walter Tull Memorial and Garden of Rest
This plaque was unveiled by the Worshipful the Mayor.
Councillor Arthur McCutcheon
on Sunday July 11th 1999
on behalf of the Sixfields Anti-Racism Forum

to Commemorate the siting of the
Walter Tull Memorial
Dedicated to the life of a hero
A symbol of hope against all forms of racism.'

Walter's name is commemorated on the **Folkestone Civic War Memorial**, the town of his birth. The memorial was unveiled by Lord Radnor on Saturday, 2 December 1922 at the eastern end of the Leas and it was dedicated by Canon Tindall. Although slightly misty, it was dry and not a particularly cold day, which went a long way in ensuring a large crowd turned out to attend the ceremony. Lord Radnor had served during the First World War as Brigadier General of the Dehra Dun Brigade in India, between 1914 and 1917.

A lot of time and effort had gone in to organising the event to ensure that it went as smoothly as possible. The mayor and many other notable local dignitaries were there, as well as some from France, Belgium and Italy. The relatives of the 578 local men who had died during the war were provided with a special enclosure, which allowed them to be close to the proceedings. Many of the town's voluntary organisations for adults and youngsters alike, helped line the approach to the memorial. A military guard of honour was provided by men from the 1st Battalion, Oxfordshire and Buckinghamshire Light Infantry.

Such was the size and closeness of most communities then, that there were not too many people not affected in some way by the loss of those who had died serving their country. For many it was because they were related, whilst for others it was because they were neighbours, friends or work colleagues.

Most of the country's war memorials were erected and unveiled between the years 1920 and 1922, and most were paid for out of public donations. There was no official government criteria as to how or why an individual should be commemorated on a war memorial. In some cases the same individual was included on two or three local war memorials. By way of an example, Billericay in Essex blends into the two nearby villages of Little and Great Burstead which are literally a stone's throw away from each other. Each location has a war memorial with some of the names appearing on all three.

War memorials were extremely important to all communities no matter how big or small they were. During the First World War if a man died in a foreign theatre of war, then that is where he was buried, meaning that a memorial was quite often the only place that families could visit to remember and mourn those whom they had lost. After the war was over, most people did not have the financial means to travel abroad and visit the actual grave of the person they had lost. Today, if a soldier is killed, no matter where that might be, their remains are always sent back home to the family, which usually means they have a grave or some kind of location where they can go to mourn their loss and remember their loved one. This was not the case during the First World War. A man was buried close to where he fell in action or died of his wounds, this is why there are comparatively few graves of the fallen from that war to be found in cemeteries or churchyards throughout the UK.

A record of the unveiling of the Folkestone Civic War Memorial appeared in the *Folkestone Express, Sandgate, Shorncliffe and Hythe Advertiser* newspaper dated Saturday, 9 December 1922. When unveiling the memorial, Lord Radnor made a short speech congratulating those responsible for it:

> *'Erected as it is in the first place to the memory of those who belong to Folkestone and who fell in the war, one's first thought on an occasion of this kind is the very deep and very sincere sympathy with the relatives of those who fell, and that sympathy is all the deeper and more sincere because, I suppose, there is hardly one of us who has not lost a dear relative or any rate, a dear friend during those four and a half years. Lastly this memorial reminds us of those hundreds of thousands of men who passed this way on their way to the Front.'*

Walter Tull's name also appears on the **Dover War Memorial**, not because he was born there, nor because he lived there, but because his mother was born there and her family were Dovorians as well. His name is also commemorated on another war memorial in Dover, which stands in the churchyard of St Peter and St Paul church.

The Dover War Memorial has somewhat of a poignant story attached to it. The memorial is immediately outside Maison Dieu House, which over the years has had many different purposes. It has been a residential home, a library, the Borough Engineer's offices, a Navy Victualler Office, and is currently home to the Dover Town Council. The memorial is a bronze figure of a youth, which apparently is 'symbolic of self-sacrifice and devotion'. The sculptor was Richard Reginald Goulden, who designed other First World War memorials in numerous locations across the United Kingdom. As a younger man he had also studied as an art student in Dover.

The British Army's Medal Rolls Index for the First World War, shows Goulden had served during the First World War as a second lieutenant, then a lieutenant and finally as a captain in the Royal Engineers, and that at least one of the sections in which he served had been a Territorial unit. They also show that he was awarded the 1915 Star, the British War Medal and the Victory Medal, all of which were not applied for until 3 October 1929. He had been Mentioned in Despatches for his work on the Western Front.

He was a married man who lived at 425 Fulham Road, Fulham, London, with his wife Muriel Olive Cecile Goulden and their daughter Wilma Ruth Goulden. When he died on 6 August 1932 he left £2,616 17s 9d in his will.

A war memorial erected to commemorate the names and lives of local men lost in a bloody and barbaric war always had pride of place within the community, but for it to have been made by a man who had fought in the same war gave it more poignancy and meaning. This aspect was enhanced even more with the unveiling of the memorial by Vice Admiral

Sir Roger Keyes, who has so many military awards and letters after his name, he was like a walking alphabet. He was accompanied by the Archbishop of Canterbury. The ceremony took place on Wednesday, 5 November 1924 with a guard of honour in attendance from the 2nd Battalion, Green Howards Regiment. The men stood to attention with their polished rifles to the fore with bayonets attached, as they paid homage to their fallen comrades. Other regiments from the infantry, the artillery as well as Territorial units, were also represented.

When I see photographs of such occasions I imagine a large group of men sitting unnoticed in the background somewhere, out of sight, dignified, not one of them making a fuss. Who are these men? In the case of the Dover War Memorial, they are Walter Tull and all his comrades who were killed during the First World War, taking part in the proceedings and looking out for their loved ones.

As well as the 721 names that appeared on the memorial at the time of the original unveiling, another fifty-five men were also honoured on the same day by Sir Edwin Farley, who had been the Mayor of Dover during the years of the First World War. Also present were the then Mayor and Mayoress, Mr and Mrs R.J. Barwick. The fifty-five men in question had been held by the Germans as prisoners of war and released at the end of the war. The men and their guests were provided with tea and cakes and listened to some short speeches made by Sir Edwin, the Mayor, the Mayoress and Miss Boyton, who was the Honorary Secretary of the Dover Prisoners of War Committee. In reply, Captain Donaldson expressed the thanks of the ex-prisoners of war to their hosts.

It has been said that war memorials fulfil two main purposes. Firstly, they are the result of the desire felt by most people to record, in some fitting and permanent way, the gratitude felt towards those who nobly sacrificed their all to save their country from becoming the vessel of an unwanted foreign power. Secondly, it fulfils a desire to acknowledge and show sympathy towards those who suffered, and in some cases still do, from a sense of personal loss.

The purpose of memorials is not to celebrate a victory in war, but rather to mourn the loss and commemorate the names of those individuals who died so that a victory could be gained over an aggressive nation who wished to take away our country's freedoms and liberty. The cessation of a war that was not wanted in the first place is reward enough.

Sources

www.ww1playingthegame.org.uk
www.britishnewspaperarchives.co.uk
www.cwgc.org

Wikipedia.
www.ancestry.co.uk
www.bbc.co.uk
www.spartacus-educational.com
www.1914-1918.net
https://greatwarlondon.wordpress.com/tag/black-history-month/

Index